For Laura

a fell

on the Road to Happy

Destiny.

Best Regards

Jim McNally

2 - 2 - 21

Jim M.

the YELLOW DIRT ROAD

ISBN 978-1-54399-689-0 eBook 978-1-54399-690-6

FOR MARY, my wife of forty-seven years,
who taught me about unconditional love.

"Our steps will always rhyme."

CONTENTS

INTRODUCTION 1

THE FARM 3

OUR HOUSE 11

POLIO 13

EDUCATION 19

    COLLEGE 21

    CONTINUING EDUCATION 23

    ABOUT EDUCATION 24

    ABOUT POLITICS 24

    ABOUT RELIGION AND SPIRITUALITY 26

    GUIDES FOR LIVING 26

    ABOUT PREPARATION 27

    ABOUT WORK 27

"THE LAW IS A ASS" 28

    LAW OR SAUSAGES 34

    NO GOOD DEED GOES UNPUNISHED 41

FAMILY 43

    MOTHER 43

    "JOHNNY, I HARDLY KNEW YE" 45

    MARY ELLEN 47

    BROTHER JOHN 48

    SISTER JEAN 50

    SISTER JEANETTE 52

TRAVEL 54

    EAST BERLIN 54

    IRELAND 55

CONTENTS

MARRIAGE AND FAMILY 59

    MARY ELIZABETH 59

    MARY DURKIN 60

    MARY MARGARET 61

    ELLEN 62

    DOUGLAS 62

ALCOHOLISM 64

AFTER BOOZE 71

SPONSORSHIP 77

ART 81

RELIGION AND SPIRITUALITY 84

    TRUST ALLAH, BUT TIE YOUR CAMEL 86

ACKNOWLEDGMENTS 88

INTRODUCTION

As I near the end of my life, it seems important to record some of my experiences, not as a professional writer but as a man who has had an exciting and difficult life and wishes to leave some trace of it behind. Part of my motivation for writing this book is the wish that some of my ancestors had written a few lines telling us what it was like to leave Ireland at a young age 150 years ago and sail for America, a wild and turbulent place where hardship and adventure awaited them. Since they left no record, we have only a few oral traditions of doubtful authenticity.

In the case of my mother's family, the Brennans, we have little idea where in Ireland they originated. On my dad's side, his mother came over from County Clare, having at age fifteen left a thirty-acre farm that she described as "gently sloping down to the silver Shannon." She landed at Buffalo, New York, where she was employed by Judge A. R. Wright as a domestic servant. By Grandma's account, Judge Wright was an honorable man. Doubtless she shared her opinion with my father, her only son, who influenced me to seek a career in law.

The only disclaimer I shall make is that the recollections contained in this book will not be flawless, but I shall endeavor to the best of my ability to state them as they occurred. Any inaccuracies, exaggerations, omissions, or misrecollections are mine alone.

THE FARM

There was a yellow dirt road that ran from Sioux City, Iowa, to the terrible forty-acre "farm" where I was raised. Some really poor land existed in Iowa. We had all of it. In winter, the road was frozen ruts; in spring, bottomless muck; and in summer, ankle-deep dust. It was especially dusty the year I was born, 1934, which was the year of the great "dust bowl" when it rained not a drop for months, and the wind darkened the sky with blowing dust.

The county graded the road occasionally, but whenever it rained or the frost went out, it became impassable. My mother used to say we "tore the guts out" of several cars trying to traverse that treacherous two miles of dirt between our farm and the nearest pavement. We managed to dig a meager living out of the place, but the dust eventually seeped into our souls and turned to grit.

The farm, as we optimistically called it, was originally eighty acres of yellow clay hills which Grandfather M. received as the booby prize when a Sioux City bank folded up in 1907. He lost all of the ten thousand dollars he had deposited days earlier, which represented the proceeds of two farms he had owned near Spencer, South Dakota. The story was that Granddad went down to the bank with his pistol to retrieve his money. The banker said, "You may as well shoot me, because I don't have your money; however, we will give you this good eighty-acre farm north of town."

Eventually Dad sold half of the land, leaving us with forty acres of virtually unproductive clay on which we struggled to make a meager living. Some years the crop money would just pay the taxes on the land.

We tried to raise some corn and alfalfa hay with little success on soil that was practically devoid of nutrients. We might get thirty bushels of corn to the acre when Iowa farmers generally were getting one hundred. Dad finally joined the Sioux City Fire Department for economic survival. He served there for twenty years, twenty-four hours on and twenty-four hours off, retiring as a captain. Had he not joined the fire department, we would have been really poor.

Part of the land was kept in pasture for the dozen or so rangy cattle we raised. The cattle were often discovered in the neighbor's cornfield because our fences were so poor that they would barely support their own weight. On one occasion, Dad proposed to remedy our fence deficit by building a one-strand barbed wire electric fence. The theory was that the cattle would approach the single strand of electrified wire, touch it with their noses, receive a shock and stay within the pasture. Our cattle had apparently not heard of the theory, for when the fence was complete, Dad yelled at my sister Jeanette and me to "cut 'em loose." We did, but not before whipping them on their rear ends with our cattle whips, which startled them into charging down the hill and through the new fence that might as well have been a cobweb. In the cloud of dust at the bottom of the hill, we could dimly see our father jumping up and down on his hat.

The farm as well as the family was really managed by my mother, a strong, attractive woman whose hair was gray by the time I came along. She had a good head for business and could squeeze more mileage out of a dollar than anyone I had met. Every year she planted a large garden and canned one hundred quarts of fruits and vegetables. She raised chickens and pigs and even sold sweet corn to the local markets. Mother was a marvelous cook and baker. On Sunday after mass, she would kill two chickens, pick and clean them, place them in the oven, boil and mash a lot of potatoes, make a large bowl of salad, stir gravy, cook vegetables, create fluffy cloverleaf rolls, and perhaps "whip up" an apple pie. The taste and smells of those delights are with me today.

Dad did a lot more than his share as well. Despite his short, stocky frame, he was a powerful man who could work hard all day. Once he spent days with a shovel digging a cylindrical hole in the ground probably twelve feet deep and twelve feet across. He poured a concrete floor and stairway and laid up glazed tile to make a perfect cylinder with a domed top that was three feet below the ground level. In this "cave" we stored wagonloads of potatoes, carrots, and turnips. These would more than last through the winter, and the potatoes left over would be cut up for seed. In the summer, we children would play in the musty coolness of the cave, which also served as a tornado shelter.

Money was always short. We could not afford a tractor, so we farmed the horses. The implements we used were old and had been repaired many times. We had a horse-drawn plow, a corn planter, a disc, a harrow, and various other horse-drawn devices we hadn't even named. One was a horse-drawn grader we called a "slip." It was like a big scoop with two handles at the rear, something like a wheelbarrow without a wheel. The horses would pull it along until the scoop filled with earth, drag it to where the earth was needed, and then the operator would lift up the handles and dump the load.

Our horses were a bit wild. One pair, a team of whites, ran away with Dad while he was harrowing up on the high hill behind our house. I looked up and saw a cloud of dust caused by the galloping horses and harrow bouncing behind them followed closely by a second cloud caused by Dad being dragged on his belly refusing to let go of the lines. He was cursing,

"Whoa, you sons of bitches. Whoa," he said. One need not wonder where we kids got our stubbornness.

Occasionally one of the horses would get sick, but we never called a veterinarian. When Charlie, one of our work horses, foundered on a five-gallon bucket of oats that someone had accidentally left near his stall, Grandma "dosed" him with a quart of linseed oil in an attempt to create a laxative effect. I was told to "keep him moving," which I did for a whole day, at the end of which Charlie dropped over dead.

Farming is dangerous work. It is a miracle that one of us kids was not killed or seriously injured on the farm. When we stepped on a nail, Mother would pull it out with pliers, wash the wound thoroughly with Ivory soap and water, and douse the wound with mercurochrome or hydrogen peroxide. We gave no thought to tetanus, and I do not recall ever having a tetanus shot as a child. Perhaps we created the greatest danger. We were not skilled farmers or plumbers or carpenters, but because of our financial situation, we sincerely believed that we had all these skills, and we were stubborn.

One day my brother John (we called him Buzz) and I were herding some of our cows back through a hole they had made in our fence. All but one old rangy cow went back through the hole. John and I were on either side of the hole. When she shied away from the opening, John threw his claw hammer full force at her rear end but missed and hit me in the forehead. I went down "like a polled ox" and was out for maybe three minutes. No one called the doctor. Instead, they applied wet, cold cloths to my forehead. To this day, my siblings will slyly suggest that my odd behavior results from that blow.

Sometimes we imported the danger from town in the form of my first cousin Terrance Taggart. He and I were "camping" at about age nine in our backyard near the hen house. We needed eggs to boil, and Terrance was dispatched to the hen house to gather a few. Fearing the chickens, he brought along a torch of rolled-up paper to hold under the nest to frighten them. Of course, the straw and nest took fire, and soon after, the chicken house was "fully involved," as the firemen would say. When the fire truck came followed by legions of neighbor kids, we went right on camping, ignoring the whole scene. Doesn't everyone have a little fire once in a while? Our guilt was transparent in spite of our pathetic attempt to frame Dick Hadley, a neighbor kid who was slightly delinquent.

A more serious Terrance event occurred when we were about ten. We were playing with small boats in a large washtub out behind our house when Terrance without warning threw a large wooden duck decoy, hitting me in the back. Stunned and frightened and enraged, I chased him past the barn, hurling a three-tined pitchfork at his back. It stuck deep in the barn, narrowly missing him as he ran by. I know for sure it would have gone clear through him powered by a rage I did not know I had. It would be many years before that deep rage dissipated.

Of course, farming was not all hard work and danger. My four siblings and I had many ways to entertain and amuse ourselves. We owned two old bicycles, several used sleds, two pairs of primitive skis, various pairs of ice skates, and the old type of roller skates that clamped on your shoes. We had bows and arrows, .22 rifles, and a couple of 12-gauge shotguns. Some toys we could not afford, so we made them, sometimes quite expertly. During the Second World War, Brother Buzz built a 50-caliber machine gun that strikingly resembled the real thing. Our poverty compelled us to be creative.

In summer, we often walked two miles to Leeds, a suburb of Sioux City, where we swam in the public pool, or we swam in the Floyd River, a treacherous, muddy stream named after Sergeant Floyd, who was the only person to die while serving in the Lewis and Clark expedition.

In winter, we played ice hockey with tree limbs and beer cans. Our hockey rink was a large pond in the hills surrounded by scrub oak trees that sheltered it from the wind. The still water froze smooth as glass, ideal for skating.

At the edge of the pond, we would build a large fire to warm our feet and comfort our wounded. Since we did not have padding or masks or gloves, we were frequently wounded by the primitive hockey sticks. Our best winter sport was tobogganing, and our best toboggan was a twelve-foot piece of stainless steel that Dad had purchased for a kitchen counter-top. At three feet wide, it was perfect for six intrepid tobogganers. Steering was somewhat of a problem, but we took the occasional crash as part of the cost of having fun.

There were also family celebrations, which involved large numbers of relatives usually gathered at our farm because of our huge yard and because Mother, as the oldest girl in a family of eleven Brennans, was sort of a surrogate mother for her brothers and sisters. The Fourth of July was an especially grand bash at our place.

Preparation for the big day began weeks in advance. We cleaned the yard, painted the fence, scrubbed the lawn furniture, and generally "squared away" (Dad's phrase) the farm. Early in the morning of the Fourth, we ran the American flag up the pole, peeled buckets of potatoes, boiled dozens of eggs, laid in gallons of vanilla ice cream covered with dry ice in large canvas sacks, and prepared to serve sixty or seventy people a righteous Fourth of July dinner. And what a dinner it was: fried chicken or steak, hamburgers or hot dogs with sweet pickle relish, mustard, and ketchup, mounds of potato salad, fresh vegetables ripe from the garden, pickles, onions, big slices of watermelon, sweet corn on the cob, and slices of juicy, ripe tomatoes. Dessert would be ice cream and chocolate cake or apple pie. Homemade lemonade or coffee or soda was served throughout the meal.

Naturally, we all overate. After dinner, the men sat around outside in lawn chairs with their feet up, hands clasped across their bellies, smoking cigars. The women kept busy putting away the leftovers and washing the dishes and pots and pans. We children played "capture the flag" or "red light/green light" or "hide and seek" until we were exhausted. When it got dark, we captured lightning bugs in a glass jar.

Fireworks were illegal in Iowa but not in South Dakota, so we would drive over to Stevens, a small town just over the border, and load up with fireworks. We bought lady fingers, cherry bombs, rockets, Roman candles, sparklers, pinwheels, and other assorted incendiary devices that startled and entertained us all in celebration of our declaration of independence from Britain.

The only holiday bigger than the Fourth of July for us was Christmas. As young children, we did not really appreciate the religious significance of the day. To us, it was more about Santa Claus, in whom we devoutly believed, who would be sneaking in our house on Christmas Eve to leave gifts. The same ritual played out each year. After a lovely dinner, we kids would be ushered down into the basement where we sat on the rickety steps and listened to the mysterious sounds of "Santa" moving about upstairs placing presents under the tree. After a half hour of suspense, the basement door opened, and we were told that Santa had come and gone. Eyes wide, we crept upstairs to behold a dazzling array of gifts that had appeared under the tree as if by magic. Amid shrieks of joy, we tore open the presents, "oohing" and "ahhing" with delight, shouting, "This is just what I wanted!" None of the gifts was expensive, but my parents had managed to save enough to provide us with a memorable Christmas.

One Christmas when I was eight or nine, there appeared on our porch a small, white fox terrier wearing a big red bow on his neck. I named him Ernest Schultz after a colorful fireman who served with Dad. The name seemed to fit him perfectly until the day that the real Ernest Schultz came to dinner. For that day only, we summoned our pet with, "Here, Dog. Here, Dog." For twelve years, Ernie and I tramped the hills of Northwest Iowa together, camping, hunting and fishing. As a hunting dog, he was a real disappointment. One cold winter day, we were hunting ducks along the Floyd River. I had my dad's old single-shot Bay State 12-gauge shotgun loaded with no. 4 shot. As we rounded a bend in the river, two mallards flew up off the river. I fired and dropped one duck in the water. Ernie jumped, swam to the duck, clamped him in his jaws and continued on across the river to the far shore where he ate the duck. As I say, Ernie was not much of a hunting dog.

The experience of growing up on that barren farm conditioned me to take the lumps as they came and not place many expectations upon life. Add to that experience a natural stubbornness, and you create a young man who will survive some really hard years ahead.

OUR HOUSE

On the north side of the yellow dirt road, there was a three-bedroom bungalow surrounded by eighty acres of yellow clay hills. I lived in that bungalow with my parents and four siblings from birth to age twenty-nine. The outside of the house was covered with common siding interspersed with ordinary sash windows. For a wooden frame construction, it was well insulated, warm in winter and cool in summer. We heated it with a coal-burning furnace in the partial basement.

The house was entered through a long screened-in porch, which led to a large living room of the same length. Beyond the living room straight ahead were the dining room and kitchen. To the left was a hallway that led to the three bedrooms and single bath. In winter, we added storm windows over the sash windows to keep out the cold, but we were unskilled at "banking" the furnace fire, so our hardwood floors were cold on bare feet in the morning. The interior of our house was beautifully decorated. Mother had excellent taste in furnishings and a good sense of color and design. Our living room was carpeted with lovely forest green carpeting wall-to-wall. On the walls were carefully chosen prints of well-known paintings by Renoir, Monet, Van Gogh, and Klimt. Our dining room was decorated with a beautiful mahogany dining-room table and six chairs. On the north wall was a polished mahogany credenza, behind which was a striking wallpaper mural depicting a Roman villa.

While the house was a generally comfortable place to live, there was an undercurrent of tension caused by my father's uncontrollable temper. In short, you might say that he was a "rageaholic." My mother did the best she could to keep things under control, but on occasion my father would erupt, throwing things and yelling. We children learned to be hypervigilant to his moods and got very good at assessing his emotional temperature.

One winter we were snowed in for a month. Between our house and town was a high hill through which a deep cut was carved for the road. That cut blew shut with snow twenty feet deep so that even the snowplow could not come through. We did well for about twenty days. Then we ran out of coffee, sugar, and my father's King Edward cigars. I saddled my horse and rode through the snow over the hill alongside the cut and on to town, where I obtained the precious sugar, coffee, and King Edward cigars, and returned home.

Last January I returned from California to Sioux City to attend my oldest sister Mary Ellen's funeral. I had not seen the old house for many years and drove right by it, not recognizing it for the many changes that had been made. The brick pillars on either side of the driveway were gone, the old barn and chicken house were no more, and a swimming pool had been added at the east side of the house. The biggest change, however, was that the yellow dirt road had been paved, providing all-weather access to the house.

Writing about the old house has brought back a flood of memories, some pleasant, some painful, but now I can close the door on that place for the last time.

Shut the door.

It was a good house... but a long time ago.

POLIO

I graduated from Heelan Catholic High School in June of 1952 close to the bottom of my class. After graduation, I got a job pumping gas at the Blue Star Gas Station on Highway 75. In the daytime, I pumped gas, fixed tires and worked on my '35 Ford coupe hot rod. At night, I took my girlfriend to the drive-in theater. My mother said I was "burning the candle at both ends" and repeatedly warned me to get more rest because of the polio epidemic that was raging then in Woodbury County, but being seventeen years old and in love, I did not listen to her.

On August 29, 1952, I awakened in the morning with a slight sore throat and a stiff neck, classic symptoms of polio myelitis, a viral disease that kills the nerve cells that power the muscles. My parents insisted that I see Dr. Frank McCarthy, our family doctor, who conducted a number of tests including a spinal tap (which felt like someone driving a Mack truck through my spine). The results were conclusive: acute polio myelitis. I was admitted that night to St. Joseph's Mercy Hospital, where I spent 105 days. The first week, I was in and out of a coma with fever and chills.

One morning after the fever subsided, I tried to put my legs on the floor, but they would not move. At first I thought I was just weak from a fever. Then gradually it dawned on me that I was paralyzed from the waist down. The shock was massive. I became depressed. My God, what would become of me? I couldn't walk. The doctors were sympathetic but not too sensitive. One said cavalierly, "You'll just have to find a big guy to carry you around." I prayed to my childhood God. No response. I cursed and screamed and "troubled deaf heaven with my bootless cries," all to no avail. Probably I would never walk again.

My legs shrank to half their original diameter, and to keep them from stiffening, the Sister Kenny treatment was administered twice a day. This treatment, named after the Australian nurse who developed it, consisted of dropping steaming hot woolen blankets on my whole body, toe to chin. The nurses picked the blankets out of a steam kettle with tongs, as they were too hot to handle by hand, and plopped them on my body. They burned terribly. Another treatment was stretching the legs, which had already stiffened dramatically, by placing me on my back and raising one leg straight up while holding the other flat on the table. The pain was extreme. I could feel the stretch all the way up to the back of my neck.

A wonderful physical therapist, Helen Calloway, worked on us patients day and night at great risk to her own life. She had come from Chicago but could not live in the white part of town because she was black. The only other treatment was the Hubbard tank, which was filled with very hot water into which we patients were lowered on a stretcher. There, the physical therapists would move our legs and arms to keep them limber.

Boredom and despair were with me always during those long months in the hospital. I conducted wheelchair races in the hallways, usually resulting in a collision, just to keep from going nuts. I read endlessly and watched TV a lot. My sister Jean sent me wonderful books which helped to open my mind to a larger, richer world. I read *Don Quixote*, *The Brothers Karamazov*, *Crime and Punishment*, *War and Peace*, and other classics. With her encouragement, I came to believe that I actually had a working brain and a capacity to learn. My girlfriend could not visit me in the hospital, nor could any of my other friends. Fear of contagion was extremely high. Gradually my girlfriend drifted out of my life, adding to my depression.

When I had been in the hospital about ninety days, the local orthopedic surgeon came into my room and announced that he had me scheduled for surgery the next day. He said he was going to stiffen my right knee and fuse seven of the vertebrae in my back so that I would be able to walk "after a fashion." I told him where he could put his scalpel and that neither he nor any other son of a bitch was going to cut on me. I later learned that the good doctor was an alcoholic who sometimes operated on people while under the influence. To this day, I do not regret my defiance of his treatment plan.

I went home in a wheelchair that Christmas, and a sad Christmas it was. My oldest sister, Mary Ellen, had contracted bulbar polio and was recovering at home. She was left with a slight problem swallowing. My sister Jeanette had a milder case of polio from which she completely recovered.

In January of 1953, I returned to the hospital to learn to walk on crutches and leg braces. They fitted me with two long steel braces that had a shaft which ran from the heel of my shoe up to a wide leather band around my upper thigh, one on each side of the leg. At the knee on each shaft was a lockable hinge that would allow the knee to bend when the lock was released. Because my back was very weak, they fitted me with a full-length back brace, which ran from a leather band around my hips up on either side of my spine to the back of my neck. When they first lifted me to my feet, I almost passed out. It had been more than five months since I last stood on my feet. Slowly they raised me up between parallel bars, which I grasped in order to drag my legs along one at a time. It was slow going and extremely demanding. "Jesus," I thought. "It'll take me all day to get anywhere with these braces."

After several weeks, they discharged me with two full-length braces, the back brace, and a pair of full-length crutches. The rest of the winter, I sat around my parents' house visiting with friends, drinking beer, and becoming a burden to my parents. The next winter, I moved to Kirkland, Illinois, to stay with my aunt Winnie, a "take charge" person who obtained for me a lot of physical therapy and with whom I did a lot of exercises, none of which improved my legs. Still, merely because I was walking on crutches, my arms and upper body gained a lot of strength.

Kirkland was the home of the Brennan Land and Cattle Company, a loosely run corporation owned by my mother's five brothers. During the first summer there, I managed to crawl up on an HT-4 shovel, fired it up, and began operating it. The HT-4 was a crawler tractor with a large scoop on the front that was used for moving earth and loading trucks. I became quite proficient at operating that machine and worked four summers doing so while attending college.

While visiting in Sioux City, I was contacted by a man named James Taylor who worked for the Iowa Vocational Rehabilitation Department. Mr. Taylor, a mild gentleman, suggested that the State of Iowa might be willing to pay my tuition and books if I wished to attend college. Rudely I laughed at his suggestion, saying, "I barely made it through high school. What the hell would I be doing in college? Besides," I added somewhat bitterly, "I don't think I want your charity."

Jim Taylor replied evenly, "We are not offering charity, James. We would like to make you into a taxpayer."

His response struck me as so unexpected that I laughed out loud and said, "Okay, Mr. Taylor. I'll become a taxpayer." So I went down to St. Ambrose College in Davenport, Iowa, where I studied political science for three years and eventually became a taxpayer. Jim Taylor succeeded beyond his wildest dreams.

At some point during my college years, I threw away the back and leg braces, sawed off the top of the crutches, and converted them into Sister

Kenny crutches with a strap around the arm just below the elbow. Later I made a beautiful pair out of rosewood. These I used for more than fifty years through law school, the U.S. Attorney's job, the Iowa legislature, my first marriage, twenty years of a trial practice, and twelve-plus years as a Superior Court judge. My shoulder joints eventually wore out, the left one losing all its cartilage in an auto accident that killed Mary, my first wife, in 1968. In 2007, I consulted Dr. Ryu, a doctor in Santa Barbara, California, who had fixed Wayne Gretsky's shoulders. He said, "You have gone twenty years too long on those shoulders. I can't fix them, so you'll have to find another way to get around." After getting a second opinion at the University of California, Los Angeles, I bought an electric scooter and a van to carry it in. I had to park my flashy 560SL Mercedes coupe. The change was a bit of an ego buster. I use the electric scooter and van to this day, and I had plenty of ego to bust.

More devastating to me than the physical damage was the psychological impact of polio. At seventeen, I was more than a little proud of my physical power. I could ride my horse at a full gallop barebacked clamped on with only my legs. I could ice skate, swim, and run with the fastest kids. So when I awakened that day in early September to the knowledge that my legs no longer worked, the shock was overwhelming. I thought my life was over. Naturally, an uneducated, unsophisticated, naive boy like me would conclude I was no longer a man. It took many years of study, work, introspection, and living in the world to learn that the measure of a man is not the strength of his legs. One of my role models was Franklin Delano Roosevelt, who was asked when he was first elected president of the United States, "Mr. President, we are deep in a depression coming into a world war and meeting resistance to our plans from all sides. How are you going to handle all of this?"

Roosevelt replied evenly, "Well, when you've spent two years just trying to wiggle your big toe, everything else looks easy."

Amen, Frank. Amen.

The hardest part of that transition was letting go of the physical trappings of a healthy body. I sold my beautiful .22 caliber antique lever-action rifle for a case of beer and gave away a really good pair of figure skates. I could not drive a car, so I sold my sweet 1935 Ford coupe hot rod for half of what it was worth. Relationships also changed. My girlfriend, whom I took to the junior/senior prom and danced with for the first and last time ever, drifted out of my life. It was many years before I allowed myself to grieve these many losses. Somehow I just kept going a day at a time. I cannot say that life got easier. I just learned to say, "It's not bad or good; it just is."

As I look back on the sixty-plus years that I have been "differently abled," I cannot escape the conclusion that polio has been a gift to me. I know that seems completely counterintuitive. Admittedly, it had taken many, many years to reach that place. Without diminishing its extreme difficulty, my life carefully examined will reveal that I never could have learned to read and appreciate great literature and poetry and music, never gone to college and law school, never been a federal prosecutor nor a state senator nor a Superior Court judge had I not had polio. And not least, I became a taxpayer.

EDUCATION

Shakespeare had it just right: "The whining schoolboy, with his satchel and shining-morning face, creeping like snail unwillingly to school."

I was that whining schoolboy being dragged unwillingly by my mother to the first grade at the Cathedral Grade School in Sioux City, Iowa. I was five, almost six years old and frightened, a shy country boy who had never seen thirty unruly kids in one room. The teacher, Sister Clarissina, was a tiny, kindly, loving nun who referred to me as "himself." After a brief conversation with the nun, my mother disengaged my little hands from her dress, whereupon I shouted, "I'm not staying here with this old son of a bitch." Humiliated, Mother hastily withdrew, leaving me to the tender mercies of the Catholic Church. My outrageous outburst unfortunately became the keynote for my entire educational career.

Strangely, the first grade was one of the few happy periods of my education. Because I was shy and ill at ease, Sister Clarissina treated me with great kindness. Once she encouraged me to bring a butter churn to class and make butter for the class. For one brief and shining moment, I acquired some status. The rest of grade school was a blur of fear since some of the nuns were teaching a type of hellfire-and-damnation religion. Perhaps my imagination magnified their words, but the result was the same—a thoroughly frightened child. In seventh grade, I memorized the Latin of the mass staying after school because of some infraction solely out of fear.

High school was a different experience. The first year was spent at Trinity High School, an all-boys school that was staffed by the Marianist Brothers. They weren't so much preaching hellfire as they were physically giving hell to the students. I knew better than to cross one of these men, but one day I punched a fellow student's books from under his arm, which action was observed by Brother McKee. He merely picked me up by the belt and the seat of the pants and dumped me headfirst into a large garbage barrel. The punishment did fit the crime, although it was a bit unorthodox. The last three years of high school were spent at Heelan Catholic High School, a coed school, where I took on the role of class clown. My acting out soon put me at odds with the administration, which earned me numerous commitments to "eighth hour," where, after regular school hours, I was compelled to copy the dictionary. The punishment may have improved my vocabulary some but did little for my oppositional nature.

At graduation as I was waiting in line to receive my diploma, Father Lenz, the giant priest who manned "eighth hour," said to me, "M., if your diploma is signed, it will be a miracle."

My best recollection is that high school was boring, a lot of memorization, not much discussion, and a few interesting teachers. Admittedly, most of the fault was mine because I was restless, irritable, and discontented during those years. Oddly, thirteen years after graduation while I was serving in the state senate, I was invited to give the commencement address at Heelan. I recall saying to the students, "It has been just thirteen years since I sat where you are sitting, and there are teachers here who will swear that it took thirteen sticks of dynamite to get me out of this school." Still playing the clown.

COLLEGE

St. Ambrose was a small liberal arts college in Davenport, Iowa, where I spent three enjoyable years studying political science. I had no cash to speak of, so I lived in terrible rented rooms, one of which had no storm window. The snow literally drifted under the window onto the sill. I made a lot of friends there: Tom Hussey, an Irishman from Chicago and a former Marine Corps drill instructor; Frank Coulon, a seminary student from Nashville, Tennessee, who played classical music on the piano; Bob Watkins, a shambling hulk of a man and a true genius; Jack Jarrard, all-around good guy, and many others. We were an odd bunch of unlikely friends who drank a lot of beer and plotted a lot of treason against the crown.

My mentor was Dr. Matthew McMahon, head of the political science department, who inspired me to dig into political science. His lectures were hugely entertaining and enlightening. His philosophy leaned toward the left where I felt entirely at home, causing me to register for the first time as a Democrat—heresy, since my parents were Republican. They said I had gone away to college and "turned left." Dr. McMahon taught about social justice and how money has controlled politics since the beginning. He admired Harry Truman and FDR. His inspiration urged me on to a career in law and politics, which he considered honorable professions when practiced by honorable men. He described politics as "the science of the possible." He not only inspired me but helped me survive. In my junior year, he hired me to grade freshman essay exam papers, which provided me with a small but necessary income.

After three years of college, I moved over to Omaha, Nebraska, to study law at Creighton University School of Law. For about six weeks, I acted like a real law student, wore a suit and tie every day, briefed the cases, recited in class, stayed out of the bars. Then the first grades came out. I had not done well. It did not occur to me that nobody had done well. They were trying to break down our little egos so that we might be taught something. Unfortunately, I took it personally, removed the suit and tie, went back to the bars, and literally drank my way out of that good law school in less than a year.

A perfect illustration of my oppositional nature occurred at Creighton. We had a course called Bills and Notes, all about legal documents used in business. The night before the final exam that determined the grade for the course, four of us—Paul McCarthy, who wore a big leg brace; Lenny Suchanek, who was completely blind; Don Sylvester, a little drunk; and I who walked on crutches (we called ourselves the Law Firm of Halt, Lame, Blind, and Indifferent)—went to South Omaha to drink. After a night of carousing, we arrived home late, but no one remembered to set an alarm clock. When everyone is responsible, no one is responsible.

We awakened at the half-time break of the test. Frantically, we dressed and raced over to the law school. There, Professor Gottlieb, with whom I had verbally jousted all year long, fumed at us, "Where in the hell have you guys been?" To me, his attitude was condescending and demeaning. My buddies cast their eyes downward and mumbled vague apologies. I looked the good professor straight in the eye and said, "Professor Gottlieb, we decided to give these other turkeys a little head start." My little remark cost me the course. My grade was 69, just below passing. My buddies all passed and went on to graduate from Creighton Law School. I washed out and went on to graduate from the University of South Dakota School of Law.

The University of South Dakota is located in the small town of Vermillion in southeastern South Dakota "where hen shit freezes and friendship ceases," as one wag crudely put it. I enrolled in the law school there in 1959 and graduated in 1961 with an LL.B. To say the very least, USD was a laid-back place, since most of the students were from ranching or farming backgrounds and would tolerate few restrictions on their freedom. They loved to drink beer and raise hell. I fit right in.

The courses did not seem that difficult, so I applied myself diligently and got decent grades. Professor Davis and I got along well, and he gave me a good grade in constitutional law. He also invited me to write an article for the *South Dakota Law Review*. I made some good friends there—Ronnie Banks, a full-blooded Lakota Native American, top student in our class; Frank Wallahan, a bright little Irishman; and Patrick McKeever, a droll fellow and roommate during our last year.

I drove my old 1950 Ford from Sioux City, a distance of forty miles, during the first year at USD, but the last year, I shared a twenty-foot "trailer" with Pat McKeever in Plum Vista Court, a rundown trailer park near the law school.

During one two-week period that year, the temperature day and night dropped to twenty degrees below zero. Naturally, that was when our finicky heater quit. Preparing for bed, Pat put on a pair of sweatpants, Levi's, a hooded sweatshirt, a navy P-coat and watch cap, mukluks, and four-buckle overshoes then crawled under the heavy blankets. I did similarly in the other end of the trailer but still felt the cold. The finale of our Plum Vista opera occurred when I spread Drano on the top of the ice that had formed all over our bathroom floor, which was also the floor of the shower. Magically, the ice melted and went down the drain. What I did not know and regrettably learned much later was that the pipe that drained the shower also drained the toilet. More significantly, the pipe was rubber. Naturally, the Drano ate the pipe, and for the rest of the winter, all the waste from the shower and the toilet accumulated under the trailer. Of course, because of the bitter cold, the waste could not be smelled, so we did not notice. When spring came and the weather warmed, an outrageous stench began to drift from under the trailer. The landlord came and said one word: "Out."

CONTINUING EDUCATION

After graduating from USD in 1961, my education began. By this time I had developed a strong love of learning. Admittedly, it was a love that had little focus, ranging from art to music to geology to astronomy. At St.

Ambrose, Father Menke was a brilliant teacher of astronomy who sparked in me a lifetime interest in the subject. Because of that interest, I found a small meteorite in my backyard in Des Moines, Iowa, years later. I mailed it to Menke, who took it to Alcoa Aluminum Company and placed it on a spectrograph. Sure enough, it was nickel and iron, a true meteorite. I still use it as a paperweight.

Poetry has also made a deep impression in my life. My sister Jean introduced me to the work of T. S. Eliot, whose "The winter evening settles down with smell of steaks in passageways. Six o'clock. The burnt-out ends of smoky days" brings back a flood of images, and Rumi's "The eye goes blind when it only wants to see why" always arrests my attention. I have memorized a fair number of these passages, which help to maintain some serenity.

I continue to read a lot. Most of my reading is nonfiction. I have especially enjoyed *Magnificent Deception*, the story of how FDR was allowed to be presented to the public as relatively able when, in fact, he could not walk a single step, and *Legacy of Ashes*, an account of how totally inept our CIA has been. I read books by Joan Didion, Maeve Binchy, Jeff Shaara, Noam Chomsky, Tom Brokaw, Gore Vidal, Anne Lamott, and many others. It is still a wide-ranging but unfinished education. Here are some of the simple things I have learned along the way:

ABOUT EDUCATION:
- Education without understanding is like a jackass with a library on his back.

ABOUT POLITICS:
- If you can't take the heat, stay out of the kitchen.
- Never strike a king unless you are sure you can kill him.
- The enemy of your enemy is not necessarily your friend.

- The opera ain't over 'til the fat lady sings.

- "If two men agree on everything, you may be sure that one of them is doing the thinking." *(LBJ)*

- "If you've got them by the balls, their hearts and minds will follow." (LBJ)

- There are only a few inches between a halo and a noose.

- There's only a slight difference between leading a parade and running ahead of a lynch mob.

- Never get into a pissing contest with a skunk.

- Money talks; bullshit walks.

- If you like law or sausages, you should never watch either one being made.

- There go the people; I must follow them because I am their leader.

- A politician knows about the next election; a statesman, about the next generation.

- In the country of the blind, the one-eyed man is king.

- He who rides the back of the tiger will end up inside.

- It isn't the size of the dog in the fight; it's the size of the fight in the dog.

- No man's life or property is safe while the legislature is in session.

- If you are not the lead dog, the view never changes.

- Be nice to the people on the way up; you will surely meet them on the way down.

- A scorpion will not sting you because he is angry with you; he will sting you because he is a scorpion.

- Close enough for government work.

- If it ain't broke, don't fix it.

- Politics is the science of the possible.

ABOUT RELIGION AND SPIRITUALITY:

- Religion is for people who are afraid they might go to hell; spirituality is for people who have been there.

- Trust Allah, but tie your camel.

- Let go and let God.

- If you want to hear God laugh, tell him your plans.

- If it is God's will, it flows together easily; if not, you have to force it.

- God feeds the birds of the air, but he doesn't drop the food in their nests.

- A Chinese peasant will stand on the side of a hill with his mouth open for a long time before a roast duck will fly in.

- Perfect love casts out fear.

- If you turn it over to God, you ain't got it anymore.

- Ultimately enlightenment may mean simply "lighten up."

- If you get too spiritual, you will be of no earthly good.

- "There are more things in heaven and earth, Horatio, than are dreamt of in your philosophy." (Hamlet)

GUIDES FOR LIVING:

- Stay in the now.

- Live one day at a time.

- The past is guilt; the future is fear.

- "Leave a little something on your plate." (ninety-seven-year-old Great Grandmother Kirby)

- You cannot think your way into right action, but you can act your way into right thinking.

ABOUT PREPARATION:

- "Give me six hours to chop down a tree, and I will spend the first four sharpening the axe." (Abraham Lincoln)

ABOUT WORK:

- Don't start the day any faster than you expect to end it.
- Most of the world's work is done by people who don't feel well.

"THE LAW IS A ASS"*

It is not easy to trace back to the beginning of my interest in the law. Part of it came from stories my father told about a local trial lawyer he knew, Frank Sullivan, who had wonderful, persuasive powers with juries. Another part came from a book called *The Great Mouthpiece*, written by William Fowler, that I read in high school. Looking back, it was a sensational, over-dramatized account of New York criminal defense lawyer William Fallon, who in the 1920s pulled rabbits out of hats and defendants out of trouble largely with trickery and deceit. Fallon on one occasion was defending a woman accused of murdering her husband by serving him poisoned cake. Naturally, the remainder of the cake was in evidence as "Exhibit A." In his closing argument, Fallon said to the jury, "Surely if this cake is poisoned, it would kill me if I ate a piece," whereupon he grabbed a large piece, crammed it in his mouth, and swallowed it. The courtroom burst into pandemonium, forcing the judge to declare a recess. Fallon raced from the room onto an elevator down to the basement, where an ambulance and a doctor waited to pump his stomach. The woman was acquitted.

---

* Mr. Bumble in Charles Dickens's *Oliver Twist*

Of course, William Fallon became my idol almost to the gates of insanity and death. You see, Fallon was a terrible drunk who loved the theater and the actresses who played in it. I almost reenacted his life.

After graduating from USD, I was employed by a venerable old law firm in Sioux City called Crary & Huff. Ralph Crary, the founder, was a district court judge whose three sons, Bruce, Bob, and David, ran the firm. Wally Huff was a tough little man who had been a commander in the U.S. Navy. My first assignment was to examine abstracts of title to real property. An abstract of title is nothing more than a complete history of a piece of dirt, whether it be a house, a farm, or a vacant lot. The history shows every deed, mortgage, satisfaction of mortgage, judgment, lien, tax levy, or other encumbrance against the property. The abstract examiner must read every word of every page of the abstract and write an opinion as to who owns the property. Next to watching corn grow, examining abstracts is the most boring job on earth. After six months of this, I began to wonder if I wanted any part of the law.

Then Donald O'Brien, a family friend, called me from the federal building down the street. Don had been appointed United States District Attorney by President Kennedy. He said, "How would you like to be a federal prosecutor?"

I said, "Can I start tomorrow?"

Don replied, "Not quite. You have to go through an FBI check."

In 1962, I was appointed Assistant United States District Attorney for the northern district of Iowa by U.S. Attorney General Robert F. Kennedy. I was elated. Our job was to prosecute all federal crimes arising in our district and represent the United States in all civil actions arising in our district. Since there were only three of us, Don O'Brien, Ivan Hossack, and me, we had enormous caseloads. I traveled to six cities in northern Iowa to try cases of all kinds, from defending a postal truck driver on a traffic matter to prosecuting the son of New Orleans crime boss Carlos Marcello for interstate transportation of firearms by a convicted felon. It was exciting work.

It was in the U.S. Attorney's office that I learned to love trial work. A trial lawyer assumes many roles. Obviously, he is an actor. He is also a director, a producer, a writer, and even a critic. As a director, he must decide which witnesses to call, the order of their appearance, the preparation of the witness to withstand cross-examination, suggestions as to how the witness should dress, and so on. As a producer, he must be sure he has the financing to properly represent his client with the necessary experts, exhibits, photographs, testing, et cetera. As a writer, he must be constantly aware that every word spoken in the courtroom is written down by the court reporter and becomes the "transcript" or written record on which an appeal to a higher court is based.

Making a good record for appeal is an art that a good trial lawyer must master. As an example, suppose the witness says, "He shot me right here," pointing to his upper left arm. The court reporter will write, "He shot me right here." Unless the trial lawyer makes a proper record, the Court of Appeals will forever wonder where the man was shot, so the lawyer must say, "Your Honor, let the record show that the witness was indicating by pointing to the upper portion of his left arm about four inches above the elbow. Does Counsel agree?" The opposing lawyer will usually agree. Now the Court of Appeals has a complete record. Of course, the uninitiated spectator will think the lawyer is nuts for stating on the record what everyone can plainly see.

Probably it was the drama in the courtroom that most appealed to me. Every case that comes into court has a story. Sometimes they are gory, sometimes sad, sometimes boring, sometimes shocking, but every day, real-life dramas are acted out before a judge and jury. I was drawn to that drama like a moth to a flame.

There are few occupations that provide the tension that comes when a jury has reached a verdict in a murder case. The foreman hands the verdict to the bailiff, who walks slowly to the bench and hands the verdict form to the judge, who reads it carefully then hands it to the clerk, saying, "The clerk will read the verdict." Your stomach knots up as the clerk intones, "We the jury in the above entitled case find as to Count One, the charge of murder in the first degree, that the defendant is guilty as charged."

However, it is not just the verdict that creates stress. Every part of a jury trial is important, like jury selection. Once I was defending an attractive female lawyer on a drunk-driving charge. We had exercised all of our peremptory challenges (the right to excuse a juror from serving for no stated cause) and were down to a choice between an older female schoolteacher and a retired lieutenant of detectives from the Los Angeles Police Department. I said to the defendant, "This is where the rubber hits the road. We never want a cop on the jury, and old women schoolteachers tend to be very critical of young women. Do you have any sense of which one to pick?"

She said, "Does it matter that the detective winked at me?"

I said, "It matters a lot," and selected the detective, who led the jury to an acquittal.

In another case, I was defending a fireman who came home one night in an alcoholic blackout and shot and killed his wife. He woke up the next morning in jail thinking he was in for being drunk in public. A very sharp psychiatrist for the state testified on direct examination, "I believe with reasonable medical certainty that the defendant at the time of the shooting had the mental capacity to form the intent to commit murder."

Knowing I had nothing to lose, I asked on cross-examination one question. "Doctor, do you believe that at the time of the shooting the defendant actually had the specific intent to commit murder?"

The doctor paused for a long time and finally said, "I don't have enough data." That one question and answer convinced the jury to reduce the charge to manslaughter from murder.

In 1964, I left the office of U.S. Attorney and opened a small office in Sioux City, sharing space with Jack O'Brien, Don's brother, and Dan Galvin. My first major case came along in the person of Wallace Whitehead, an elderly man who was arrested for performing abortions in the Holiday Inn. A housekeeper had informed police that she suspected my client. Based on this, the police listened through the wall of an adjoining room for six hours, gathering enough information to obtain a search warrant. They served the warrant on the motel manager, who let them into Whitehead's room where he was found in flagrante delicto doing an abortion. Whitehead was arrested and charged with the felony of performing an abortion.

I made a pretrial motion to suppress evidence before Judge Morris Rawlings, who would also be the trial judge. I asserted that the defendant was deprived of his right to be free from unreasonable searches and seizures in that the warrant was served on the motel manager, a person who had no right to open Whitehead's door and admit the police, a person who had no more right to enter that room than a total stranger. Judge Rawlings's response was, "You want to do what? You want me to throw out all the prosecution's evidence and dismiss the charges? Your motion is denied." We went to a jury trial, and to the surprise of no one, Whitehead was convicted.

Later that week, I was in the courthouse law library doing some research when Judge Rawlings's bailiff came by my table and whispered in my ear, "Make a motion in arrest of judgment in the Whitehead case." I did not have to be told twice. I made the motion that allowed the judge to review all his earlier rulings. Judge Rawlings granted it, reversing all his earlier rulings. He suppressed all the evidence and dismissed the charges. He had finally read the U.S. Supreme Court decisions upon which we were relying.

The local church ministers went nuts. They rented a full page in the *Sioux City Journal* to denounce Judge Rawlings, a man of great courage who was willing to follow the law irrespective of the consequences.

A year later as a state senator, I carried Judge Rawlings's nomination to be an Iowa Supreme Court justice through the senate. He was confirmed and served honorably until his death. Sometimes the good guys win.

In June of that year, I married Mary Elizabeth Davis, a lovely woman from Omaha, Nebraska, whom I had met a year earlier while on a trip to Europe. I also filed nomination papers to run for the state senate. John Kennedy had been assassinated, and Lyndon Johnson was now the president. I did not care much for Johnson and his overbearing Texas style, but he was now at the top of the Democratic ticket on which I was now running. As Harry Truman would say, "He's a son of a bitch, but he's our son of a bitch."

My campaign for the state senate cost less than one thousand dollars, most of which we raised at a hot dog and bean feed. The balance came from a few supporters and some of my own money. I campaigned relentlessly, attending two or three church dinners around the county every Sunday. We stenciled a couple hundred red, white, and blue "M. for Senate" signs. We even nailed a bunch of the signs on the river pilings facing the Missouri River, because Barry Goldwater was going to travel up the river by barge and stop in Sioux City. We knew that there would be coverage by the national TV networks showing our signs. When he saw all the "M. for Senate" signs along the river, Goldwater was heard to say, "Who the hell is M.?" I appeared on television, radio, talked to church groups, stood outside factory gates at shift changes passing out cards, went in and out of a lot of bars and coffee shops, and tried to shake hands with every voter in the county.

I had no realistic expectation of winning. My opponent was a personal friend of the editor of the *Sioux City Journal* who arranged front-page coverage of my opponent taking one of his campaign posters off a utility pole because it was "illegal" to place them there. In addition, Woodbury County was overwhelmingly Republican. However, it was 1964, the year that Lyndon Johnson defeated Barry Goldwater in a huge landslide, carrying himself and a lot of other barely-competents into office, including me. I woke up on the day after the election hung over to find that I had been elected to the state senate.

LAW OR SAUSAGES

In January, I moved my new wife, who was pregnant with our first child, to Des Moines, the state capital. She delivered Mary Margaret on March 2, 1965, at St. Joseph's Hospital in Sioux City while we were home on recess. We could not have been happier.

Because of the Democratic landslide, both houses of the state legislature were now controlled by Democrats. We had work to do. Harold Hughes, our popular governor who ran ahead of Johnson, proposed a bill that would legalize the sale of liquor by the drink. For years and years, you could only get liquor through a state store in limited quantities—a little Republican socialism. Hughes said Iowans "drink wet and vote dry." We ended that, allowing liquor to be sold by the drink in regular bars. We also reclassified beer as a food so that it could be sold in grocery stores. Ironically, Harold Hughes was a recovered alcoholic who had not had a drink in many years.

I also cosponsored the bill that repealed the death penalty in Iowa. Otto von Bismarck said, "If you like law or sausages, you should never watch either one being made."

Amen, Otto.

I introduced a bill in the Iowa senate that required all freight cars to have reflectors on their sides to warn motorists approaching a moving train at night. For years, people were smashing into the sides of freight cars and being killed, because at night out in the country, you cannot see a train moving across your line of vision unless lights are shining through the train between the cars from the other side. It seemed to me that a simple solution would be to require all freight cars to have reflectors on their sides. Naturally, every railroad company in the United States would have to spend a little money to reflectorize their cars, because eventually every car would pass through Iowa. Of course, this was unacceptable to the railroad companies, who sent lobbyists from all over the country to kill this bill. Senator George O'Malley from Des Moines was leading the opposition, backed by a large majority of senators who had been given "campaign contributions" by the railroad companies. I was backed by a few maverick senators and common sense, much like General Custer.

Seeing that my bill had no chance of passing, I asked the senator from Des Moines if he would yield to a question. "Senator, can you give me one honest reason why this bill should not pass?"

He replied, "Yes, I can. I have the votes."

I sat down. Otto von Bismarck was right.

Because the legislature had been controlled by farmers for dozens of years, the pay was a pittance. The farmers had nothing to do in the wintertime, so they could come to Des Moines and play for ninety days. We were paid twenty-five dollars a day, plus ten dollars for secretarial service, plus one round-trip train ticket to and from Des Moines. The sixty-first general assembly in which I served lasted 175 days, a record. I almost went broke. So, moved by financial necessity and a certain cynicism about how money controlled politics, I did not run for a second term.

Back in Sioux City, I joined the Law Firm of Gill, Dunkle, Beekly & M. I had been there a short time when Bishop Joseph Muelle of the Sioux City Catholic Diocese called me, saying he would like to speak to me. I wondered what horrible wrong I had committed that would require the bishop to intervene, but I went to see him. He said that the four dioceses of Iowa were considering opening an office in Des Moines to look after the legislative interests of the church, and might I be interested in a position there. We discussed numerous issues, including money, which I sorely needed. After discussing it with Mary, I decided to go to work for the four Catholic dioceses of Iowa.

In 1966, we moved back to Des Moines. I opened offices downtown under the title Iowa Catholic Conference, of which I was the executive director. I started out by publishing a monthly newsletter called *ICC News*. I kept the dioceses advised as to matters affecting the Catholic people of Iowa, and I marshaled support and opposition for and against legislation of interest to them. The bishops did not allow me to register as a lobbyist, but that is essentially what I was.

On July 3, 1968, my wife, Mary, my three-year-old daughter, Mary Margaret, and I were traveling from Omaha, Nebraska, to Des Moines, Iowa, on Interstate 80. I was driving my old Mercury station wagon about seventy miles an hour, just under the speed limit. Mary was in the passenger seat and was not wearing a seat belt because it made her uncomfortable, she being two months pregnant with our second child. Suddenly we were struck from behind by a vehicle traveling over eighty miles an hour. It was a perfect PIT maneuver. We were struck on the left rear corner and spun around. Then we were catapulted off a high embankment and rolled over end over end seven times. My wife was thrown from the vehicle and killed on the freeway that day. Mary Margaret and I ended up upside down on fire in a dry creek bed off the road about fifty yards. Some U.S. Mail truck drivers pulled us out of that wreck. Mary Margaret was not physically hurt at all. I had a broken, dislocated shoulder, some broken ribs, and cuts and bruises, but nothing life-threatening. I was not drinking that morning. Thank God.

I spent six days in a Sioux City hospital, after which Mary Margaret and I moved back to Des Moines. I asked my mother, Mary, to join us and take care of my daughter. I was devastated and depressed and stayed drunk as much as possible.

In December of 1968, I was standing in a huge arched window in the State House Library looking down Grand Avenue, the main street of Des Moines. It was overcast and bitterly cold, spitting snow and promising a storm. I said to myself, "This is my last winter in this F'ing place." And it was. I went immediately to the national lawyer's directory, *Martindale-Hubbell*, and looked up the requirements for admission to the State Bar of California. I started a file entitled "Operation California" and began filling it with information on California. Over time, the file became voluminous.

One day in early 1969, I was sitting in the Savory Hotel bar with a former colleague, Jack Schroeder, when a fellow he knew from California walked in and sat down. He introduced himself as Bill Goergan. After a brief conversation, he said to Jack, "Our friend John Van Geldern is in jail in Ventura, California, and we need to get him a lawyer."

Jack said, "Here's one of the best criminal lawyers in Iowa right here," pointing at me. Three days later, I was on an airplane bound for Ventura, California, where I met Van Geldern in the local jail and began the process of negotiating fees. Right away Van Geldern, a tall, handsome, brilliant con man, said he only wanted to hire me to sit in the second chair and advise him while he represented himself. I gave him the usual riff about how the man who represents himself has a fool for a client. When he would not budge from that position, I told him that I would only represent him as a lawyer with full control of the case. He declined, and I flew back to Iowa. Van Geldern did represent himself and managed to get thirty years to serve.

However, in the week that I was in Ventura, I met and got acquainted with the members of a Law Firm of Danch, Ferro, Lagomarsino & Cooper. They were most generous with their time and allowed me to use their office as a headquarters. A few weeks after I had returned to Iowa, John Danch, a generous, soft-hearted Hungarian, called me and said, "You really liked it out here, didn't you?" I replied affirmatively. He then said, "How would you like to come to work with us?"

I said, "I would." Over a few days, we worked out the terms. In July of 1969, I drove from Des Moines to Ojai, California, where I bought a house, started a job as research assistant for Danch, Ferro, Lagomarsino & Cooper, and began studying for the California bar examination.

Just as I was stopped at the citrus checkpoint at the California border, the astronauts were landing in the ocean after traveling to the moon. My mother, Mary, and daughter, Mary Margaret, came to California a month later.

The California bar exam is the toughest test I have ever taken. I was eligible to take the Out-of-State Attorneys Exam, which consisted of ten essay questions of which the student could opt out of any two. This meant that attorneys who had practiced for more than four years in another state could take a one-day examination consisting of only eight questions. I had purchased an electric typewriter. Then, fearing a power shortage, I purchased a manual typewriter, but I had difficulty composing intelligent sentences and paragraphs on the manual typewriter, so in the end, I wrote the exam with a twenty-cent Bic ballpoint pen.

I never did find out how well or badly I did on the California bar exam, although that particular test had an 80 percent failure rate. When I read my name in the *L.A. Times* as one who had passed, my interest in bar exams ceased. To this day, I don't care if I passed by one point or thirty; I only know that I had never studied harder in my life. For the last thirty days before the test, my friend Mike Arkin and I went to the law office where he was working and studied for eight hours every day.

The day I went to work in Ventura for Danch, Ferro, Lagomarsino & Cooper, a young man named Ed Whipple also joined the firm. Ed was a tall, blond, surfer type of guy, smart and easygoing. We got along well from the beginning. At lunch, we would drive up Ventura Avenue to a little Mexican takeout hole-in-the-wall restaurant and buy the most delicious beef burritos, which were my introduction to authentic Mexican food. Ed and I would go down to the beach, sit on the sand, and drink our Pepsis and eat our burritos.

One day, Ed said, "You know, Jim, you and I will work our asses off for twenty-five years just so we can sit on the beach and eat burritos. Why don't we stop working right now and sit on the beach and eat burritos?" We laughed and went back to work.

After I passed the bar, I asked Eddie to join me in the practice of law. He agreed. We would split expenses and fees down the middle. We shook hands, and that was our partnership agreement. We never had a written contract. We worked together for seven years and never had a harsh word pass between us. Ed Whipple was a superb lawyer, an excellent partner, and a loyal friend. He died a few years ago of Lou Gehrig's disease.

The Law Firm of M. & Whipple took off with a bang. Lee Cooper from the Danch firm had just been appointed to the Municipal Court, so he asked me to take over a major felony case that was just in the pretrial stage. The case was *People v. Merril Shapiro*, in which the defendant, a wealthy Los Angeles garment manufacturer, was accused of hiring two thugs to seriously injure the lawyer who was representing Shapiro's wife, a former Powers model, in their divorce. Incidentally, the lawyer was also sleeping with Mrs. Shapiro. The two thugs whom Shapiro had hired muffed the job when the lawyer's secretary unexpectedly walked in on them. They were caught and agreed to tell all, making a fairly tight case for the prosecution.

In those days in California, there was a defense available known as the diminished capacity defense. If the accused could show that at the time of the offense, he was suffering from a mental disorder or defect that diminished his capacity to form the specific intent to commit the crime, he could be convicted of a lesser offense or acquitted entirely. That defense lost public support when Dan White murdered San Francisco Mayor Moscone and Councilman Harvey Milk and at his 1979 trial asserted a diminished capacity defense based on his having consumed too many Twinkies. White was convicted of a lesser crime of manslaughter, causing the public to repeal diminished capacity as a defense.

With the facts clearly against us, I decided to use the Twinkie defense, which was still available. Our expert psychiatrist was a man named Champion Teutsch, who had been treating Shapiro for years. The only problem was that Teutsch was not a real psychiatrist; he was a civil engineer whose wife was a psychiatrist. Apparently, he had seen that his wife was making a bunch of money fairly easily, so he started "treating" people as a self-titled human dynamics engineer. There was a real question of whether our "shrink" would even be allowed to testify.

Our strategy was to present Shapiro as a war hero, which he really was, having been commissioned in the field to the rank of captain by General George Patton after Shapiro's commanding officer went insane. Shapiro had commanded a number of tanks at the Battle of the Bulge and liberated several Nazi concentration camps, and being Jewish, this latter experience had a profound effect on him. As I saw it, our job was to reenact World War II in the courtroom featuring Merril Shapiro, whose horrible war experiences diminished his capacity to commit the crimes.

Surprisingly, the trial went quite well. I was able to call into doubt the testimony of the thugs, as they both had extensive criminal records and had made a sweet deal for themselves with the District Attorney, all of which cast a shadow over their believability. In addition, I had a jury that wanted to have a good time, so I entertained them for six weeks with madcap humor and outrageous tactics. As an example, when one prosecution witness was giving particularly damaging testimony, I nudged a pile of grand jury transcripts off the counsel table onto the floor with my elbow, distracting everyone away from the testimony. The jury responded by having a birthday cake placed on my counsel table, which greeted me after lunch on my birthday. You know you are not doing badly when the jury sends you a birthday cake. They loved my cross-examination of the lawyer/victim about his affair with Shapiro's wife.

Our main witness, of course, was Champion Teutsch, who testified at great length about Shapiro's experiences in the war and how he was completely traumatized by them. He went into excruciating detail about the death camps that Shapiro had liberated and the living skeletons that he had found in them. The jury was profoundly moved.

After six weeks of trial, Merril Shapiro was acquitted of all charges and walked out of the courtroom a free man. The jury had literally pardoned him in spite of the evidence. I was particularly relieved, because I knew that our principal witness would not have been able to utter a single word in court if the judge had known that he had no training in psychiatry and no mental health credentials at all. The District Attorney had just neglected to ask him the right questions.

NO GOOD DEED GOES UNPUNISHED

Bill Goergan was drunk when he left the Sportsmen's Lounge in Ventura at closing time and drove his station wagon south on U.S. 101. In the middle of town, he either blacked out or passed out, crossed the center ice plant at high speed, and hit a station wagon carrying five people head-on. All five died in the flaming collision. Bill was horribly injured. When the California Highway Patrol drew his blood in the hospital, it was 0.26, three times the legal limit. He was charged with five counts of manslaughter and five counts of felony drunk driving.

Since Bill was a kind of a ne'er-do-well insurance broker and part-time deal maker, he had no money, but because he had introduced me to the Danch firm, I felt some obligation to him and agreed to represent him pro bono, a Latin phrase that means you don't get paid. The trial had to be postponed many months because Bill had numerous broken bones, a ruptured spleen, and many other serious injuries.

After careful examination of the wreck, we found on Bill's station wagon a broken tie rod end. This would not necessarily help us; however, that tie rod end showed a rusted crack halfway through its width. So the tie rod that controlled the steering was weakened, but did it break before or during the collision? We could find no reputable metallurgist who would say that it broke before and therefore caused the crash, so we settled on an old mechanic to testify that in his opinion it did.

The trial did not last long. The prosecution easily proved that Bill was dead drunk. The only issue was whether the rusted tie rod or Bill's drunkenness caused the crash. Our expert did not stand up well on cross-examination, and to nobody's surprise, Bill was convicted of ten felonies.

A good trial lawyer knows that the opera ain't over 'til the fat lady sings. At sentencing, I persuaded Judge Willard to send Bill down to Chino, a prison reception center, for a diagnostic study, which would be a maximum ninety-day stay at the center, in hopes of getting a recommendation that Bill could be handled on local probation rather than sent to state prison. Clearly, it was a long shot.

While Bill was down at Chino, the local probation officer changed his opinion. He initially recommended that Bill go to prison; now he thought he could be handled on local probation. However, Chino did not agree. The reception center's report recommended that Bill go to state prison for the maximum term prescribed by law, twenty-five years.

At the final sentencing hearing, we pulled out all the stops. I said to Judge Willard, "Imagine a hypothetical jurisdiction where a man gets drunk and kills five people in a flaming collision. Let us suppose that the penalty was to take the defendant out and break one hundred of his bones, rupture his spleen, cut and lacerate his body all over, destroy his business, and run off his wife and two boys, leaving him with a painful, broken body, no family, and no way to make a living. You might say that such a punishment is pretty harsh, but that punishment has already been inflicted on Mr. Goergan. What would it gain society to lock him up in a steel cage for twenty-five years?" To everyone's amazement, after only eighty-seven days at Chino, Judge Willard placed Bill Goergan on five years felony probation with no additional jail time. The fat lady had sung.

But the title of this case is "No Good Deed Goes Unpunished." A year after the trial, Bill went back to Iowa and told one of my lawyer friends that I had really screwed up his case. My friend said, "He sure did. What did you get? About seventeen days per dead body?"

FAMILY

MOTHER

At age seventy, my mother was living alone in our old farmhouse when a large woman carrying a double bitted axe entered our front porch and began using it to pry up the sash window to enter our living room. My mother was on the phone with my sister when she saw the window being raised. "Just a minute, Mary Ellen," she said evenly. "Some damn fool is trying to get in the house." Mother put down the phone, hurried to my old bedroom and took down Dad's old 12-gauge single-shot shotgun. Placing a shell in the chamber, she cocked the weapon and aimed it at the head of the intruder who was now halfway in the house. "If you come in the house, I'll blow you across the road," Mother yelled. The woman, seeing her life about to end, retreated and ran down the road, leaving the axe behind. Mother called the sheriff, who arrested the woman and returned her to the mental institution from which she had escaped. This incident tells a lot about my mother's courage and attitude.

Mary Loretta was a country girl, the oldest of eleven children whose mother was somewhat ineffectual; therefore, my mother really raised her siblings, and they treated her with great respect. Among her many skills was the ability to cook, sew, garden, and raise chickens. On Sundays after mass, she would kill two chickens and pick and clean and bake them. She would make mashed potatoes and gravy, coleslaw, and vegetables followed by apple pie and coffee, all from scratch.

She sewed many of her own clothes, including a fancy cloth coat with a fur collar. We five children, of whom I am the youngest, knew that Mother was in charge. Her technique for getting discipline was to withhold love. If you crossed her, she would give you the cold shoulder for days. She often said, "I know how to give people a good letting alone."

While her schooling did not go beyond high school, it was really quite extensive. In her last year of high school, they translated Latin and Greek poetry, and she could quote Shakespeare at length. Her favorite: "There is a tide in the affairs of men, which taken at the flood leads on to fortune; omitted, all the voyage of their life is bound in shallows and in miseries."

From the time I was a little boy, Mother and I would argue. We argued about politics, religion, farming, the weather, everything. I began to wonder why we were always arguing. In college when I studied psychology, I reached a shallow conclusion that our arguments had a Freudian significance. That conclusion was not satisfying, but I held onto it for a long time. In the last few years, I have slowly seen another side of these arguments. When I was a young boy, I was very sensitive and shy. Mother knew that if I went out into the world with that stance, the world would eat me alive, so I now believe that she set out to toughen me up for the real world. She would put me up against her five redneck cowboy brothers, who were absolutely ruthless in their teasing of the children. In fact, one day in 1942, Uncle Mike, a fat man who had received exemption from military service for being "essential agricultural labor," was mercilessly teasing my brother, John, about not being in the service. "Why don't you get a gun, Johnny? Huh? Huh?" My brother was seventeen.

I shot back from the other end of the table, "Or John, maybe you could get an exemption from military service as essential agricultural labor and not have to go to war at all like Uncle Mike." That remark hit Uncle Mike like a two-by-four. He got up and left. He could dish it out, but he couldn't take it.

As the result of Mother's constant debating with me, I became a pretty effective debater and eventually a competent trial lawyer, state senator, and Superior Court judge.

"JOHNNY, I HARDLY KNEW YE"

My father, John Edward M., the only child of James and Bessie M., was a rageaholic and had a lot to be angry about. His early years were spent on a homestead near Spencer, South Dakota, which was still wild country in the early twentieth century. His mother was frightened by the Native Americans and frightened by her husband's fighting with the neighbors to the point where she threw his six-shooter down the well. (This was gun control, circa 1907.)

One day while the old man was farming down the road, two young Native Americans rode up to the house on their ponies, got off, came in, and sat at the table. They wanted food, so she fed them. They ate the food and got up and left. She said that she also had a hot poker heating in the wood stove just in case they wanted something else. She was quite wise.

With respect to the neighbors, one Saturday night four neighbor boys with a big team and wagon came down the road and knocked all my grandfather's brand-new fence posts out of alignment with the wagon hub. The next morning was Sunday, and the boys came down the road to go to church. The old man was out in the road with a six-shooter, saying, "Today we're going to fix fence, boys." He got them out of the wagon, and they spent the entire day fixing the fence.

Eventually my grandmother persuaded my grandfather to leave South Dakota. He sold the farm in 1907 and set out for southeastern Iowa, where he expected to buy a farm with good black soil. As the little family rode away from the homestead in a horse-drawn wagon, my father's little dog, his only companion, followed along until it became apparent that he was being left behind. It broke my father's young heart to see his little friend stop following the wagon.

My grandfather, being an alcoholic, had to stop over in Sioux City Iowa, a wild frontier town, to wash the alkali dust from his throat with some good whiskey. He deposited ten thousand dollars from the sale of the farm in a Sioux City bank, which failed three days later. Threatening the banker with another pistol, he demanded the return of his money. The banker said, "You'll have to shoot me, because I don't have your money, but I will give you this wonderful eighty-acre farm north of town." Grandpa took the deal and tried to farm the eighty acres of yellow clay hills, which he did with marginal success.

Physically, my father was short and stocky but extremely strong. He could work all day in the hot sun, stopping occasionally to drink water from a one-quart milk bottle. During World War I, he served as a torpedo man first class on board the USS N-3, a 140-foot-long submarine. On one occasion, his sub was towed out to sea near the Azores to do battle with a German U-boat recently sighted. As they were towed, they repaired one of their diesel engines. Having reached the area where the U-boat was sighted, they were lying in the moonlight charging their batteries when a British convoy emerged from the fog bank led by a battleship that bore down upon them.

Sighting the N-3, the British captain thought it was a U-boat, and he ordered a U-turn. As the ship heeled over, turning, he fired a six-inch deck gun. The explosive shell skipped across the water like a pebble across a pond and struck the N-3 amidships at the waterline. Instead of exploding, the shell penetrated the hull and lodged smoldering between the inner and the outer hulls. Declining assistance from the British and cursing the captain, Commander Dibrell limped his sub back to New London.

After the war, my dad had an opportunity to study law in a lawyer's office, but his old parents insisted that he come home to work the marginal farm. He always regretted not studying law. Sometimes I think I lived out his dream.

It soon became obvious that the farm would not support his family and five children, so my dad took a job in the Sioux City Fire Department as a fireman, where he stayed for twenty years, retiring as a captain. Despite the courage and discipline it took to sail on the N-3 and lead men into burning buildings, Dad had enormous difficulty controlling his temper. Oddly enough, in a major crisis, he could be calm and focused, but a broken shoelace would set off a major shouting and throwing episode.

Over the years, I have studied psychology and heard the testimony of hundreds of experts on the question of childhood anger. I have concluded that all that is necessary to make children very angry is to deprive them of enough unconditional love. That was the fate of my father.

MARY ELLEN

My oldest sister, Mary Ellen, was born during the inauspicious period between the end of the Roaring Twenties and the beginning of the Great Depression. From the beginning, she was a star, with abundant red hair and the hated freckles, and she could dance and sing in the manner of Shirley Temple. Top in her class all the way through high school, she was offered a four-year tuition scholarship to Briarcliffe College, but she could not accept because we did not have the money for lodging, food, or transportation. The first of us five children to leave home, she moved into Sioux City to live with my mother's mother and work as a secretary for a lawyer named Edith Forsling.

Because we were strict Catholics, we were required to attend Catholic schools, which were ten miles away downtown in Sioux City. Ordinarily, our mother would drive us in our old 1938 Chevy, but fairly often we would take the electric trolley that ran downtown from Leeds, a suburb two miles from our farm. One of my fondest memories of Mary Ellen comes about when I would walk downtown from Cathedral Grade School and stop at Mary Ellen's work on the way to the trolley. She always had at least twenty-five cents for me to spend as I wished. I usually would buy a toy soldier at Kresge's five-and-ten-cent store and maybe a double-dip strawberry ice cream cone. At that time during the Second World War, a quarter would actually buy something. She had several boyfriends and eventually married a gentle man named Richard Wigton with whom she had seven smart, witty children.

Mary Ellen's gift to me was her eternal optimism. She smiled easily and had a kind word for almost everyone. We would rib her about her optimism by quoting a poem, "Angus McCloud" by Ogden Nash. Angus McCloud was grateful for everything to the point where his wife stuffed a tea-tray down his throat, and "He remarked from the floor where they found him reclining, 'I'm just a McCloud with a silver lining.'" Our final taunt for which I think she has forgiven us was, "If you place Mary Ellen in a room full of horse manure, she would say, 'There's got to be a pony in here somewhere.'"

Mary Ellen died two years ago following a fall that broke her hip. In the hospital, she contracted pneumonia, from which she died. I'm grateful to have known her.

BROTHER JOHN

From an early age, my older brother, John, has been a natural engineer. Before he went to the navy during the Second World War, he built a wooden model of a 50-caliber machine gun that looked remarkably authentic. In the last few years, he has created a functioning harp and for my wife and me two beautiful burial urns made from black walnut. Numerous other fine objects have been created by him. When I went on the bench in 1982, he created a beautiful gavel and striker. The handle was made from an old shovel my father wore out, the head was a part of a poster bed of my parents', and the striker plate was part of an oak toolbox my great-grandfather carried on the Great Northern Railway.

Born at the end of the Roaring Twenties and before the Great Depression, he grew up on our marginal farm, which was all work and little production.

We called my brother "Buzz," a mispronunciation of the word "brother" by my oldest sister, Mary Ellen. He was a stocky fellow with red hair and the hated freckles.

His work life covered more than forty years, starting in the Sioux City stockyards tending cattle and ending as the head of the department overseeing the defense of product liability cases for Caterpillar Tractor Company in Peoria, Illinois. Through more than forty years, he worked as a mechanical engineer with little formal training; however, the relatively modest life of an engineer does not nearly capture my brother's life. When he worked in the Sioux City stockyards, he was butted and pinned against a water trough by a 1,600-pound bull who was trying to squeeze the life out of him. The only way he could escape was to shove his thumbs into the eyes of the bull, which backed off enough to allow him to escape. Once when he worked for Caterpillar, he was flying over Alaska in a small plane when they were hit by a blizzard that forced them to land on a lake in the wilderness. Walking inland, they found a car parked on a country road. Breaking the wing window, they were about to commandeer the vehicle when the three hunters who owned it walked out of the woods carrying high-powered rifles. My brother and his friends had to give some real explaining to the men they were about to abandon in the wilderness during a blizzard.

Brother John was also a pilot. After the war, he used his GI bill to take flying lessons. Then he bought an old double-wing open-cockpit plane made by the Stearman Company. After flying numerous flights and after several crashes, he hung up his wings and has not flown an airplane for many years.

On top of all these actions, he has also married a lovely woman named Margaret Duffy and raised nine great kids.

I've always admired my big brother, but I haven't ever told him so until now. In our family, there were never expressions of love or approval. As the British say, "It's just not done." A startling example of our emotional aridity occurred when my brother was going off to war. At the train station, John was about to board the train. Our dear mother shook his hand and said, "John, don't take any wooden nickels."

So sad.

Many years later, John and I were tent camping by Lake Powell over by Las Vegas. As we sat by the fire, John said, "Jim, did you know we raised ourselves?"

I replied, "I knew that, John, but I did not know you knew it."

That insight captured the essence of our growing up.

SISTER JEAN

Jean was a fine doctor, specializing in internal medicine. She is also my older sister, four years older than I. We were not close as young children but grew much closer as adults. We had one very large thing in common: our alcoholism.

When I was drinking, I would call Jean at midnight my time, three o'clock in the morning her time, and ask her, "Do you think that I'm an alcoholic?"

She would reply, "Of course not. How could you have done all the things you've done with your life?" What I did not know was that my learned advisor was an alcoholic.

Years later, after I was sober two years, she called me on the phone and said, "Jim, I hear you are calling yourself an alcoholic."

I said, "Yes, Jean, I'm calling myself an alcoholic because I am one."

Ever the intellectual, she asked, "What is your definition of an alcoholic?"

I replied, "An alcoholic is anyone who drinks more than his doctor does."

She said, "That's not a damn bit funny."

I said, "I think it's very funny."

I sent her a copy of the Big Book of Alcoholics Anonymous, which she read and then entered recovery. She now has forty-four years of sobriety. To this day, I am proud and pleased to have helped my sister achieve sobriety, especially since she was my guardian angel during the dark years after I contracted polio in 1952.

Jean graduated from Iowa University School of Medicine in June of 1955. She obtained an internship at St. Vincent's Hospital in Greenwich Village, Manhattan. There, she was required to ride the back of the ambulance to the scene of suicides. When some poor soul had jumped from a high building, a doctor was needed to pronounce them dead.

On one occasion, she rode up to the scene of a "jumper" only to be greeted by a large Irish cop who shouted as he held back the crowd, "Jesus Christ, are you the doctor?"

Jean shot back, "Jesus Christ, are you the cop?" She was plenty tough.

After her medical school and internship, she specialized in internal medicine and practiced successfully for more than thirty years.

Early in her career, she met and married Peter Carbonara, a young orthopedic surgeon. They had a spectacular wedding in Rome followed by a lavish reception in New York City paid for by Peter's Uncle Frank.

At the reception, I asked Peter's mother some questions about Uncle Frank, who was a black-shirt-and-yellow-tie kind of guy. "Mrs. Carbonara, what does Uncle Frank do for a living?" I asked naively.

In her broken English, Mrs. Carbonara replied, "Uncle Frank does something in the city that makes him very wealthy."

Peter and Jean had four brilliant children, Peter, Paul, Mary, and John, all of whom are bright, witty, intelligent, and successful. As I write this, my dear sister Jean is suffering from some type of dementia. She lives with Peter in Englewood, New Jersey, and has some significant problems with her memory. I am extremely sad for her.

SISTER JEANETTE

My sister Jeanette was tall and beautiful with honey blond hair and the hated freckles. Shy and quiet, she would be described by psychologists as "the lost child."

Two years older than I, she and I were fast friends growing up. We rode horses together and roamed the hills of northwest Iowa, but as we grew up and my alcoholism got worse, we grew apart.

When I was two years sober, I called her on the phone to make amends, which is part of my recovery. I said, "Jeanette, I treated you badly during my drinking years, and now as a part of my recovery from alcoholism, I am calling to make amends to you."

She said, "It sounds like bullshit to me."

Of course, my amends were premature. That relationship healed eventually over time, but we were estranged for many years.

I can only describe Jeanette's life as sad. She married a mild-mannered fellow named Joe Smith and gave him five children. They lived—if anyone lives—in Fargo, North Dakota. Joe died of a heart attack at an early age, and Jeanette died of cancer several years later.

I now see Jeanette's life as the product of an emotionally arid upbringing. She truly was the lost child. When Jean was practicing medicine in Manhattan, she invited Jeanette to New York to try out for some modeling jobs. It seemed like a good idea as she was tall, blonde, and attractive. She did a few modeling jobs but was too shy to undress in public as the work required, so she chucked the modeling career and returned to the Midwest.

After her husband Joe died, it was learned that he had taken out a loan for fifty thousand dollars from a local bank. The bank's attorney called and demanded the money. Jeanette called me to ask if she actually owed it. I researched the law of North Dakota and found out she did not owe the bank a dime. In spite of my advice, she paid them every dime, expending almost all of her cash. I was furious. Later, she called to ask me if I would help her find a lawyer to sue the bank's lawyer for malpractice. I told her to find somebody else to ask since she had no faith in my legal opinion. This was a clear example of a scared Catholic, compelled to pay every "jot and tittle" or risk going to hell.

I wish Jeanette were here today.

TRAVEL

EAST BERLIN

During the summer of 1963 I was traveling in Europe, having wangled a job as assistant tourmeister on a young-adult tour. The Cold War was still on, and East Germany was still a communist country, hostile to the United States. At the time I was employed as Assistant U.S. District Attorney for the northern district of Iowa, the equivalent of a KGB official if I were employed by East Germany. So when we landed at Tempelhof Airport in Berlin, I had to be careful. The people at the mission thought it would be safe for me to travel into East Berlin if I left my justice department credentials in West Berlin and took only my passport and some East German marks. I boarded a bus on Friedrichstrasse and traveled east toward the famous Berlin Wall, which had been erected two years earlier.

Just before the wall, we entered a large "catch pen" surrounded by high concrete walls where the East German police searched the bus and even looked under it with mirrors. Two menacing characters got on our bus, one a large man who looked like Sidney Greenstreet wearing a trench coat, the other a short man wearing a khaki uniform and carrying a "burp" gun that he pointed at my face while repeating, "Passports. Passports." Naturally, I gave him my passport, which he examined carefully for what seemed like a long time. Slowly, he handed it back to me. We then drove through a zigzag passageway bordered by high concrete walls apparently designed to prevent a vehicle from speeding through the checkpoint. At the end of the zigzag was a massive iron gate that had to be raised and lowered electrically.

The gate was raised, and we slowly entered East Berlin. I was astonished. It was nothing like I had expected. East Berlin was a gray ghost town. As far as your eye would carry down a street, there were no cars and almost no people to be seen. Maybe one or two.

The most memorable sights were the churches. All of them of every denomination were boarded up, doors and windows, with plywood, and more startling, tall weeds were growing along the roofs and the rain gutters, and tall weeds were growing in cracks in the steps. Surprisingly, however, the lawns were meticulously maintained right up to the foundations. God was indeed dead or at least overgrown with weeds in East Berlin.

As we passed back through the Berlin Wall, I felt a sense of physical relief that turned to joy when I saw Checkpoint Charlie coming up, manned by U.S. GIs wearing their distinctive steel helmets, smiling and waving us through.

IRELAND

In June of 1987, my wife Mary and I spent a month vacationing in Ireland. Around noon one day, we drove to the hamlet of Killadysert, stopping at the "phost" to buy stamps and ask about Paddy Maloney, the present owner of Grandma M.'s farm. The "phostmistress" was a summer substitute and did not know him, so we went next door to St. Michael's Church, which Grandma attended as a child. The place reminded me of another St. Michael's at home, not an altogether pleasant memory, so we hastened outside after taking a few pictures.

An old man appeared in a doorway across the street. My wife, Mary, agreed to ask him if he knew Paddy Maloney. He did. Paddy lived next door. We knocked, not expecting the welcome we would receive. When Maire Maloney opened the door, we told her who we were and that we had come to find the farm where my grandmother, Bessie, had been born. She seemed pleased and ushered us in to meet Paddy, a short, wiry, white-haired man whose pale blue eyes seemed to miss nothing. We repeated our story to Paddy and watched him warm to the idea of becoming our local guide to distant genealogical history. After stuffing us with ham sandwiches plastered with butter, he drove us in his own "cair" to Ballynacragga, the thirty-acre farm he had purchased twenty years earlier from one Cudahy. Later that day, we learned of the suspicious circumstances under which the Cudahys had inherited the property from Paddy Edwards, my grand-mother's brother, the last of the Edwards family.

Guiding his little "cair" along the narrow blacktop road, Paddy chattered about the Edwards clan and particularly about Paddy Edwards. "A fine man he was," he chirped. "You know, the cross over his grave has been toppled. I think it could be reset for about ten pounds." Our driver was casting, but I did not take the bait.

Several miles from Killadysert, we turned off the main road into a pasture, passed through some iron gates, crossed another farm owned by the MacMahans, and topped the rise that looked down on the Edwards farm and the wide Shannon River below. The view was exactly as Grandma had described it: "Thirty acres of meadow gently sloping down to the wide silver Shannon." Across the river, you could see the farms, irregular patches of intense green, stretching for miles to the hills beyond.

I thought of my grandmother not as the bent, withered crone of my childhood but as a young girl who ran and played on these lush green hills by the Shannon River. These images flooded upon me as we walked down toward the moss-covered gray stone cottage where Bessie Edwards was born. Now it was a cow barn. Its thatched roof had been replaced with corrugated steel. "It's not much now," piped Paddy, "but it was a fine house. A fine house it was."

He showed us the doorsill "flagstone," a flat gray slab of limestone into which a depression had been chiseled near the doorframe. The lower end of the doorpost turned in that depression, serving as a hinge. The door was gone. Remaining now was just the opening that admitted the cattle, which were sheltered inside.

"The sitting room was here," Paddy went on, sweeping his arm toward the east end of the long, low room. "And there," he gestured, "was where the fireplace was laid." I imaged a hot "torf" (peat) fire, the only source of heat warming the entire house. Outside, Paddy picked four apples from a scraggly tree and presented them to us with some ceremony, which concluded with, "Now we'll go and see Josie Clancy."

The Clancy farm adjoined the Edwards place and was inhabited only by Josie Clancy and his brother. As we entered the dirt track leading up to the house, Paddy Maloney whispered to me in a conspiratorial aside, "Probably we could get that cross put up right for maybe twenty-five pounds." I nodded that I understood, wondering what caused him to think the traffic would stand fifty dollars.

Josie greeted us warmly and climbed with difficulty into the back seat. His face carried the evidence of many bouts with "the crayture." He told us that he was one of twelve children; that he had spent his eighty-plus years right here on this farm. The Edwards family in his eyes were all saints. One of the girls he recalled cooked a goose and carried it across the field in a large pan covered with a white cloth. Apparently they were very short of food when the goose arrived. "But I knew Paddy Edwards well," he went on. "I was there the night he died." When pressed for more detail, he hesitated and then let fly, "The damn Cudahys got the farm. They guided his hand on the will." He then told us that the Cudahys were part of Grandmother Edwards's family. When I asked Josie if he thought Paddy Edwards was alive when they "guided his hand on the will," he said, "I don't know, James. I don't know," and lapsed into silence. Then we shook hands all around and drove away.

Our last stop was the little cemetery where Paddy Edwards is supposed to be buried. It was next to the ruins of an ancient stone church and contained no more than one hundred graves. One of them had been marked with a tall, marble Celtic cross that had fallen from its pedestal. "I think I could arrange to have this cross set back up and a little gravel spread around here for, say, fifty pounds," Paddy announced as we approached the alleged Edwards grave.

"No doubt," I replied, smiling at the steady rise in my apparent financial condition.

Back in Killadysert, we resisted the offer of more food. As we were getting in our rented "cair," Paddy made his final pass. "You know, James, one hundred pounds would right that cross and put that grave in fine condition, it would." After some very low-key negotiations, I gave him ten pounds.

Driving away, I said to Mary, "We may be the fifteenth American couple to have paid for resetting that cross." But no matter, it was a small price for the tour of Ballynacragga and the tale of Josie Clancy.

MARRIAGE AND FAMILY

MARY ELIZABETH

My first wife, Mary Elizabeth, was a tall, attractive, very bright bru-nette woman. I met her on a trip to Europe in 1963. I had wangled my way onto the tour as an assistant tourmeister, which I was barely qual-ified to be. We traveled through sixteen countries in sixty days. The tour was organized by a Catholic monsignor named Behrens. Over the time we were on the tour, Mary and I became well acquainted and continued to date, she in Omaha, Nebraska, and I in Sioux City, Iowa, after we returned to the United States.

Mary was an eighth-grade schoolteacher in Omaha, Nebraska. Her father was a battalion fire chief on the Omaha Fire Department. My father was a captain on the Sioux City Fire Department. We both came from mid-dle-class families.

A year after we met, we were married, on June 6, 1964, at St. Bridget's Catholic Church in South Omaha, Nebraska. Soon after, Mary became pregnant with our first child, Mary Margaret, who was delivered during a recess in the legislature on March 2, 1965. The day she was born, we were having a major snowstorm in Sioux City. Mary had a long labor but was profoundly happy when Mary Margaret, a very healthy baby, was born. We were both ecstatic.

Mary was an excellent mother to Mary Margaret and took exceptionally good care of her. When Mary was killed in the accident on July 3, 1968, my young daughter and I were devastated.

MARY DURKIN

The first time I saw Mary Durkin making a ten-minute talk at the Rodeo Drive AA meeting, I was sorely smitten. She had black hair and big blue eyes and a gorgeous figure. After the meeting, I asked her out to coffee. With the consent of her sponsor, she agreed to go. We had a lovely dinner at the Hamburger Hamlet up on Wilshire Boulevard. She had her ten-year-old daughter, Ellen, with her.

We began talking on the phone and dating back and forth between Ojai, California, where I lived, and her home in Westwood. It was an intense romance and courtship. We just knew that the other was the exact right one. After eighty-two days of courtship, we were married on December 3, 1971.

At the time, I thought I was still a Catholic, and therefore, I had to be married by a Catholic priest. Mary had been divorced and was ineligible to be married in the church, so we went to Watts, California, and were married by Father O'Neill. We spent part of our honeymoon at the San Ysidro Ranch in Santa Barbara in the Geranium Cottage, which was $71 a night. Today it is more than $1,500 per night.

Mary moved from Westwood to Ojai with Ellen, leaving Doug, her twelve-year-old son, in Los Angeles to finish the eighth grade. With a few bumps along the way, we have been married happily for almost forty-eight years.

MARY MARGARET

Our youngest daughter, Mary Margaret, was doted upon by me and her two grandmothers when I met Mary Durkin. She had two televisions and all kinds of things, but she did not have a father. Her father was drunk in the bar almost every night for several years after we moved to Ojai, when I could have been there for her. I still carry some guilt about this.

When Mary Durkin came along, she gave Mary Margaret chores to do and put some discipline in her life, which caused me to resist. I was used to spoiling my child and resisted any discipline.

Mary Margaret took to her new life very well. While she was in high school at Villa Nova, she got a job at the St. John of God Monastery in Ojai washing dishes. She would get up at dawn every day and ride her bicycle several miles to do her job. At graduation, she was valedictorian of her class and won numerous awards. We teased her by saying, "Couldn't you have left a few awards for the other kids?" After high school, she attended the University of California at Davis, getting a degree in agricultural economics. Then she obtained a master's degree and finally a Ph.D. in the same subject. Throughout, she has been an outstanding scholar.

Somewhat skeptically, we asked Mary Margaret what she planned to do with her degree in agricultural economics. She said not to worry; there were plenty of jobs for a person with that degree.

How right she was. And how naive we were. She is now the chief financial officer of the veterinary medical school at U.C. Davis, one of the best veterinary medical schools in the world. We could not be more proud of her. In addition to her academic life, Mary has been married to Steve for about twenty years. Steve is a bright, scholarly man who has a Ph.D. in ecology and works for the U.S. Fish and Wildlife Service. They have a brilliant son, Benjamin, who is in his last year at Claremont College in Claremont, California. He wants to be an economist. Ben is also a world-class swimmer.

Mary, Steve, and Ben are a great joy in our lives.

ELLEN

Mary's daughter, Ellen, was ten when I met her. She was smart and happy and wanted to be a part of a new family. She agreed to be adopted by me, and Mary Margaret was adopted by Mary Durkin. Ellen was always a good student, helpful around the house, and never gave us a bit of worry as she was growing up. She graduated from Chico State University and obtained a master's degree in social work from the University of Southern California. After working a few years in social work, she married a lawyer named Tom. She had two boys, both of whom have been quite successful. The oldest boy, Thomas Jr., got a master's degree in accounting as did his younger brother, Tim. Thomas went on to work for a national accounting firm. Tim went on to obtain a law degree from Southern Methodist University, where he graduated summa cum laude and was inducted into the Order of the Coif. Both boys are brilliant and real gentlemen. Ellen and Tom are ideal parents.

Whenever Mary or I have had a significant medical problem, Ellen has flown out to Santa Barbara from Austin to be there for us. She and I have spent many hours together in hospital waiting rooms. We call ourselves "The A Team."

I am most grateful for all the help Ellen has given us over many years.

DOUGLAS

Doug was twelve years old when I met his mother in Westwood. At that young age, he was already a streetwise kid who ran a large paper route.

When he came to Ojai, he got a job stocking shelves at Bayless Market. He played football as a lineman at Nordhoff High School. He was a big, tough kid.

After high school, he got a job as a firefighter for the U.S. Forestry Service out of Ojai, fighting forest fires on the ground swinging a Pulaski. After that, he got a job with the State Fire Marshal's office, where he was asked to compile a book on high-rise fire safety. When the fire marshal lost his job because of politics, Doug was head-hunted by First Interstate Bank as a high-rise fire safety expert. After all, he had written the book. After a few years there, he was head-hunted by Compaq Computer Corporation, where his work expanded more into the human relations field. After ten years there, he went over to Apple Computers as a personnel manager. His latest job is head of human resources for Sun Power Corporation, a company that manufactures solar panels as a subsidiary of Total, a French oil conglomerate.

When he was finishing college at Bozeman, Montana, Doug met a petite Italian woman named Nancy Cacciatore. Shortly thereafter, they were married and produced three bright kids: Lisa, Christie, and Mathew. Lisa and Christie now are married and have children of their own. Doug has always had a strong work ethic, starting early in the morning and working late at night. By any measure, he is an outstanding husband, father, and businessman.

ALCOHOLISM

The first time I got drunk, I was visiting my cousin in town. I lived on a forty-acre patch of unproductive clay hills called a "farm." It was around Christmastime, and we had the candy and the peanuts and all the stuff that goes with Christmas. I found a quart of sloe gin in my cousin's house. After eating half a pound of Spanish peanuts, I drank the quart of sloe gin. Then I stuccoed my cousin's house on the inside.

The last time I got drunk, I was living in Ojai, California. I had just closed the Firebird Bar and was having a late dinner consisting of a cold chicken leg out of my refrigerator. There, I found a quart of Mogen David wine, which I promptly consumed. I found myself lying on my back on the kitchen floor vomiting straight up in the air and trying to dodge whatever was coming down. Those are the bookends of my drinking life. Hundreds of drunks occurred between those two, but I count those two as the first and the last.

I loved the bars and drank in bars halfway around the world. Bar drinkers talk about three things— military, sexual, and athletics conquests. Most of it is B.S. When I was in the Iowa senate, I drank every night with the legislators. My new wife was baffled that there was so much legislative business conducted at night. When I was Assistant U.S. Attorney, the only thing that really changed about my life was that I was now falling off much better barstools. Before that, I was drinking in the old beer bars with the wooden seats and the brass rails that will hurt your ribs when you fall on them. Altogether, I drank for twenty-five years from age twelve through age thirty-seven. I loved beer and Scotch whiskey (or anything that contained alcohol). At first my experiences consisted of weekend parties where we would get someone old enough to buy us each a quart of beer, which we would drink fast and act drunker than we really were. At the last of my drinking, I would sit in the bar from five thirty in the evening until two a.m. and drink one beer or Scotch whiskey after another, staying in the bar until closing time every night.

Alcohol was the centerpiece of my life around which everything else revolved. I would accept an invitation to your house for dinner but would not show up if I thought you might not serve alcohol. I had very few friends who did not drink. I liked people who drank the way I did—voluminously.

The first time I considered that alcohol might be a problem was when I was a lobbyist and began having blood sugar problems and highly elevated cholesterol. I was also seeing little things out of the corner of my eye, and when I would turn suddenly to see them, they were gone. I consulted local doctors in Des Moines, but I did not tell them the truth, so they did not give me a definitive diagnosis. Instead, they sent me to the Mayo Clinic in Rochester, Minnesota. Those good doctors asked me a dumb question: "How much do you actually drink?"

I gave them a dumber answer: "I have an occasional social drink." After three days of testing, they came up with a tentative diagnosis. I asked, "What do you think is wrong with me, Doc?"

"We are not really sure," the doctor replied, "but we think you may have executive stress syndrome." I was relieved to hear that, because they were not referring to alcohol or abstaining from alcohol.

"What do you do for executive stress syndrome?" I asked.

The doctor said, "We have these blue pills, ten-milligram Valium tablets. You seem anxious at times, so when you get anxious, take some of these blue pills." I felt anxious all the time, so I took them all the time. If you drink a lot of alcohol and take a lot of Valium, some days you will get very serene to the point where you will not be able to hit your rear end with either hand.

The morning my wife was killed in a car accident, I had not been drinking, but I had horrible survivor guilt, and my drinking accelerated exponentially thereafter.

In 1969, I moved to Ojai, California, from Des Moines. I did not have a license to practice law in California, nor did I really know anyone out here, but it seemed like a good idea at the time. It is said that the United States are tilted slightly to the southwest, so that eventually everything that's loose rolls out to California. I spent a lot of time in the Firebird Tavern in Ojai while preparing for the California bar exam. I also worked as a law clerk for the Danch firm in Ventura. After getting licensed in California, I began practicing criminal law in an old frame house along with my new partner, Eddie Whipple.

In spite of drinking every night in the bars, I had a substantial amount of success as a criminal lawyer. After I had been drinking in Ventura, I avoided the California Highway Patrol or police or any law enforcement personnel while driving back to Ojai in the evening. I was afraid that one of those good people would stop me with a blood alcohol of 0.25, which is where I liked to drive, so I would sneak back to my office in Ventura and sleep under the large wooden conference table I used for a desk. In the morning, I would crawl out from under the desk, unshaven, fully clothed, suit and tie, sick, sorry, and hung over.

One day I crawled out from under that desk and picked up the Ventura paper, in which there was an article about the Serra Retreat House that had partially burned in a fire in 1970. The article said that the retreats were now being held and the buildings were being rebuilt. Further, you could call a number and arrange to make a retreat. Having run out of altitude and ideas (the definition of a plane crash), I called the number. A nice woman answered the phone and said, "Yes, we are having retreats, and you could come any weekend." Then she paused and said, "I was going to offer you this weekend, but this one is for alcoholics."

I said, "I'm not an alcoholic, but I will come anyway."

Keep your options open as long as you possibly can.

On the next Friday evening, I drove to Malibu and up that crooked road to the Serra Retreat House. Outside were twenty-five or thirty men who were smiling and laughing and having a good time, but they did not look like alcoholics to me. They did not have the watery eyes, the shaky hands, the unsteady gait I had seen (and displayed) so many times. They welcomed me, and on Saturday night, they invited me to the AA meeting. I said, "I'm not an alcoholic, so I wouldn't have any reason to go to an AA meeting."

"Come on anyway. You might learn something you could use in your practice," they said. They were also a little slippery. So I went to my first AA meeting at a round-table discussion with twenty-five or thirty men.

I was astonished to hear them talking about things we bar drinkers never discussed. They spoke of night terrors, waking up at three a.m., sitting up with the hair standing on the back of your neck and having no idea what you were afraid of. They spoke of "geographical cures" for alcoholism—going from one state to another, one woman to another, one job to another, running away from ourselves. In short, they were reading my mail.

When it came to my turn around the table, I spoke the most important words I have ever spoken in my life. I said, "My name is Jim. I am an alcoholic." I did not fully believe it, but I had said a lot of things in my life I did not fully believe. "He's not guilty, Your Honor. He's just the victim of a thin tissue of circumstantial evidence pasted together to deprive him of his liberty."

After the meeting, two old-timers approached me. Today I call them the good cop and the bad cop. The bad cop said, "I think you'll drink some more, but we have screwed it up so you won't enjoy it anymore."

The good cop said, "Don't pay any attention to him. If you think you might have a little drinking problem, when you get back to Ventura County, go to some AA meetings and see if there is something that will help you there." They were both right. I went back to Ventura and did what every alcoholic will do who does not have a program. I got drunk.

Soon after, I got sick enough and tired enough to reach out for help, so I called Bud G., who was a counselor in the courts and a twenty-year sober member of Alcoholics Anonymous. I said to Bud, "Bud, I think I might have the beginning of a little drinking problem."

He said, "We know."

I said to myself, "How in the hell could they know?"

It's hard to be the town drunk and not have somebody find out about it.

"What do you think I should do about my little drinking problem, Bud?"

He said, "You need to go to an AA meeting today."

I said, "I'm kind of busy today, Bud."

He said, "You're not busy. Today."

"Where would I go?"

He said, "There's a meeting in Oxnard at the Norman and Cooper Manor." It sounded pretty good to me. *To the manor born.*

I drove my dinged-up alcoholic Cadillac to the Norman and Cooper Manor. It was the worst nightmare a newcomer could have, a ramshackle old building housing twelve or thirteen old apostles wearing their blue terry cloth robes and their paper shoes. They were seated around a scarred wooden table over which was hanging a fly-specked light bulb. The head leper was reading from a blue book, and he was saying, "If you want what we have and are willing to go to any length to get it, then you are ready to take certain steps."

I said to myself, "If I don't get out of here in a minute, I may get what he has," so I left, and I went back to Bud. I said, "Bud, why did you send me to these people? They are rowing with one oar in the water." He was not pleased with my reaction to the meeting.

He shot back, "They have meetings for big shots in Beverly Hills." Then he started to walk away.

I said, "Where in Beverly Hills would they have these meetings for big shots, Bud?" He was kind enough to come back and tell me about the Rodeo Drive group of Alcoholics Anonymous.

The next Friday night, I drove eighty miles to the Rodeo Drive group. When I rolled up there, I noticed the Maseratis and Lamborghinis and Mercedes-Benzes and, inside, very fancily dressed people, even actors and actresses I had seen in films and on TV. In my phoniness I said, "This is about the way AA ought to be."

If you are so phony that you have to drive eighty miles to a fancy AA meeting, it's okay. Beats dying of alcoholism.

I started attending the Rodeo Drive group on Fridays. On the fourth occasion, there was a gorgeous brunette with big blue eyes and a gorgeous shape giving a ten-minute talk at the podium. I knew that she had what I wanted and would go to any length to get, so I asked her out to coffee after the meeting. Surprisingly, she went, bringing her ten-year-old daughter with her. We met at the Hamburger Hamlet on Wilshire Boulevard and had a lovely dinner. We began talking on the phone and dating back and forth. Eighty-two days after we met, we got married.

It turns out that marriage is not a cure for alcoholism. I continued to drink even after Mary and Ellen moved up to Ojai. Doug came later, after he had finished the eighth grade.

Somehow, I had gotten the idea that it was a "do-it-yourself" program. Of course, I had been doing it myself all my life with very little to show. I had gone to priests and psychologists and various shamans to find out what was wrong with me, but no one had an answer. Eventually, I gave up trying altogether. I said, "If I am going to be one of those losers they talk about in AA, at least I'm going to have some fun while I'm here," so I went back to the bar and continued to drink.

Toward the end of my drinking, I was representing a young man in San Diego who had been accused of importing some non-habit-forming marijuana into the United States. I was so sick that I could not drive to San Diego from Ojai (about two hundred miles) all in one day, so I stayed overnight in Malibu just to rest. In court in San Diego, I asked the U.S. Marshal to ask the judge if I could remain seated during my presentation since I was not feeling well. The judge agreed, so I sat during my presentation. On the way home from San Diego, for some reason I stopped at the ruins of the old Mission San Juan Capistrano. I knelt down at the old altar after lighting a candle and said to no one in particular, "I don't know what the hell I'm going to do." A week later, I was at the Serra Retreat in Malibu.

After the retreat, I was going to the Firebird Tavern almost every night. This went on for months. Then on March 30, 1972, I walked into the Firebird and ordered my favorite beer. They did not have it, so I ordered a bottle of Coors, which I did not like. I drank the first bottle and half of a second one. Having drank one-half of the second bottle, I shoved the second half back on the bar and walked out of the place, never to have another drink of alcohol to this day. As of this writing, that was forty-seven years ago. Today I believe that a power greater than myself removed from me the obsession to drink alcohol and has never returned it.

AFTER BOOZE

After I had my last drink, on March 30, 1972, my life got worse. For years, I had been taking ten-milligram Valium pills for anxiety. My new friends in AA said, "We don't take anything that is mind or mood altering."

I said, "Surely you could not be talking about Valium."

They said, "We are specifically talking about Valium." So I threw away my Valium and became hugely anxious. I would have anxiety attacks that would land me in the emergency room thinking I was having a heart attack. These anxiety "fits" as I called them lasted for two and a half years after I had my last drink. Mary had taught me to breathe into a brown paper bag, apparently to equalize the blood gases, which prevented me from passing out. I never took any more mind- or mood-altering drugs after that.

Over time and very slowly, my life leveled off, becoming much calmer. I was still trying one murder case after another as a defense attorney, but I was much better able to handle the stress. And more frequently,

I was asked to speak at AA conferences around California and around the country. Slowly things got better.

After ten years of sobriety, I was looking around the courtroom one day and noticed that the only person who seemed not to be doing much was the judge. I said to myself, "That would be a good job to have. He seems not to be doing much of anything." So when there occurred a vacancy on the Superior Court in Ventura County, I applied to the governor's office for appointment.

I had no realistic expectation of being appointed, but the AA people just said, "Do the footwork." I mailed seven hundred letters to the law-yers of Ventura County asking them to support my candidacy. I obtained letters of recommendation from my old boss in the U.S. Attorney's office, Don O'Brien, who was by now a federal judge in Iowa, and I got a letter from Charles Manatt who was then the National Democratic Party chair. I received a final letter from Harold Hughes, who had been governor of Iowa when I was in the legislature and was now a United States senator. I filled out a thirty-three-page questionnaire in which I said I was a sober alcoholic in AA for ten years and sent it off to the governor.

The governor, Gerald Brown, sent a commission consisting of four lawyers, two men and two women, to question me about my alleged qual-ifications for this job. After two hours that seemed to go well, one of the lawyers said to me, "You say you're sober ten years in AA. How can we be sure you will not show up drunk some Monday morning?"

I thought about the question for a while and answered, "I cannot promise you that I will not show up drunk some Monday morning, because when I was making promises like that, I always showed up drunk. I can-not make that promise, but if I continue to do what I have been doing as faithfully as I have been doing it for the past ten years, there is a reasonable chance that I will not show up drunk. That's as good as I can tell you." My next immediate thought was, "This rigorous honesty bullshit just cost you that job."

Well, it did not. I was appointed by Jerry Brown on December 31, 1981, and served until April 15, 1995, when I retired.

Governor Brown knew that I had represented a group of migrant laborers in Iowa when I practiced there. When he called me New Year's Eve of 1981, he said, "I'm going to put you on the Superior Court in Ventura County."

I said, "Thank you, Governor."

He said, "Don't forget the migrants."

Serving as a Superior Court judge was the best and the worst job I've ever had. My anonymity lasted about a week. I was serving in juvenile delinquency court where we deal with minors in trouble with the criminal law. A sixteen-year-old came up for a probation review. I had seen him around AA for over a year, and I knew he was doing well. I took him off probation. He said, "May I come up to the bench and shake your hand?"

I said, "Sure."

He came up to the bench and shook my hand and turned to a courtroom full of people and said, "Thanks, Judge. I'll see you at the AA meeting tonight."

I said, "So much for anonymity."

That revelation changed my relationship with some of the people in the courthouse. The district attorneys thought I would give away the farm, the public defenders thought they had a patsy, and various other people reacted differently, but I just kept doing what I had been doing all along.

Whenever I saw an alcoholic coming before me, I would try to get them some real help. For example, in dependency court, I would order an alcoholic parent who was abusing a child to attend three or four AA meetings a week under a "godfather" deal they could not refuse. If you miss a meeting, you do a weekend in jail.

One woman who had been leaving her young children in an overheated car for four hours while she was having some cold ones in the bar said to my bailiff, Eddie, after I had made her the deal, "I'm not going to those fucking meetings."

Eddie LeClaire, my bailiff, said to her, "I don't think I would take that attitude. He's serious about those meetings."

She came back a week later and had not gone to any meetings. I said to the bailiff, "Take this woman into custody. She owes us a week of weekends starting right now." Oh, my God. It was like I had pulled her right arm off.

She said, "I can't do fourteen days in jail."

I said, "You didn't hear me when I said you had to go to those meetings."

She did her fourteen days and came out a different person. She went to the meetings, got sober, and got her kids back. Sometimes gray bar therapy works.

The most significant thing I learned in twelve and a half years on the bench was never to make a decision until you have to. Naturally, that seems counterintuitive, and it can be called procrastination. What I learned was that when you take all the time you have, whether it is ten minutes or ten days, you will never second-guess yourself. Most importantly, your subconscious will have more time to work on the problem.

The toughest case I had to decide was the case of *People v. Kevin Kolodji*, involving a twenty-year-old man who was horribly schizophrenic. He had escaped from the county hospital where he was recovering from 125 self-inflicted stab wounds. Out on the streets, he was wearing a hospital gown labeled "St. John's Hospital" and one leather leg restraint. He was knocking on doors hoping he could take a shower. The police were called, and when they talked to him, they saw he was mentally ill and called the watch commander, who said, "He doesn't have any warrants or wants on him, so let him go." So they let him go. He continued knocking on doors and finally came to the home of an old woman whose ninety-year-old husband had gone down to the corner to get her a donut, leaving her alone. She must have frightened Kevin. He stabbed her to death with a kitchen knife.

Both the district attorney and the public defender waived a jury trial and agreed to let me try the case without a jury. I found Kevin guilty of second-degree murder but then had to decide the question of whether he was legally insane.

After Dan White had gotten away with murder in 1979, murdering Mayor Moscone in San Francisco under the "Twinkie" diminished capacity defense, the outraged public reinstated the "M'Naghten" rule, which says that you are legally sane unless at the time of the crime you are "unable to distinguish between right and wrong."

With a courtroom full of mental health advocates, I found Kevin to be sane at the time of the crime. He had hidden the knife under a pile of boxes in the front hall closet, which told me he knew that he had done something wrong. I hated that decision because he was clearly mentally ill. I said on the record I thought the law was archaic and unjust; however, I could either enforce it as I had taken an oath to do or hang up my robe and walk out of the courthouse. I chose to follow the law.

After twelve and a half years on the bench, I began to experience extreme pain in my shoulders and additional muscle weakness. The diagnosis was post-polio syndrome, a condition that occurs in many polio patients thirty years after the acute onset. I consulted with Dr. Susan Perlman at UCLA Medical Center, who advised me to get out of the high-stress business of being a judge. She said, "You have used the few muscles you have left as if you are running behind enemy lines."

On April Fools' Day of 1995, I hung up my robe for the last time and walked out of the courthouse. That day, my only thought was, "Is that all there is to a career?" My loyal and excellent secretary, Vicki Villegran, and superb bailiff, Eddie LeClaire, organized a grand retirement party that was attended by more than one hundred people.

Since my retirement, I have continued to sponsor twenty-five people in AA and speak whenever I'm asked around the country, averaging about once a month. Our children are all grown and married and have children and grandchildren of their own.

In 1998, Mary and I sold our lovely home in Ojai and bought a cottage overlooking the ocean in Santa Barbara. We live there happily, having found in the words of AA cofounder Bill Wilson "a quiet place in bright sunshine."

SPONSORSHIP

In AA it is common for new members to find a "sponsor." That is a person who will introduce them to the program and guide them through AA's Twelve Steps.

In some parts of the country, sponsorship is considered to be of the utmost importance, particularly in Southern California. Whereas having a sponsor is not mandatory for members of AA, it has proved invaluable for many. Chapter 11 of a "conference approved" book called *Living Sober* states, "Not every AA member has had a sponsor. But thousands of us say we would not be alive were it not for the special friendship of one recovered alcoholic in the first months and years of our sobriety."

I have had five good sponsors: Bud G., David H., Dick H., Eddie C. and Jim F. Each of them gave me a slightly different take on the program, but all of them were very helpful. My last sponsor moved to Florida twenty years ago, so I have not had a sponsor since then. I feel that if you cannot learn the program from five good sponsors, you're probably not going to get it.

In some cases, the sponsor prides himself on total domination of the "sponsee." They call themselves "Nazi sponsors." I like to remind them that I am old enough to remember the real Nazis for whom we had a perfect solution—a 30-caliber round through the forehead.

The true AA approach is that we "share our experience, strength and hope with each other in order that we may solve our common problem," as the AA Preamble says. And as the Twelve Traditions state, "Our leaders are but trusted servants. They do not govern." I like to say that the highest rank I will ever attain in AA is sober.

I have sponsored quite a few people, as many as twenty-five at a time. My approach is very nondirectional. I treat my sponsees as adults and rarely give an order unless I see them heading for a cliff. I usually say at the beginning of our relationship, "My objective is eventually to become unnecessary." I have had a small part in helping people get sober, but I do not take credit for it. Sponsors should be more like a beggar telling another beggar where he has found some bread.

"Probably no human power could relieve our alcoholism." That includes sponsors. The only program we have to create sobriety is the Twelve Steps of AA. For those who are not familiar with them, here they are:

1. We admitted we were powerless over alcohol; that our lives had become unmanageable.

2. We came to believe that a Power greater than ourselves could restore us to sanity.

3. We made a decision to turn our will and our lives over to the care of God *as we understood him.*

4. We made a searching and fearless moral inventory of ourselves.

5. We admitted to God, to ourselves, and to another human being the exact nature of our wrongs.

6. We were entirely ready to have God remove all these defects of character.

7. We humbly asked God to remove our shortcomings.

8. We made a list of all persons we had harmed and became willing to make amends to them all.

9. We made direct amends to such people wherever possible except when to do so would injure them or others.

10. We continued to take personal inventory, and when we were wrong, promptly admitted it.

11. We sought through prayer and meditation to improve our conscious contact with God *as we understood him*, praying only for knowledge of his will for us and the power to carry that out.

12. Having had a spiritual awakening as the result of these steps, we tried to carry this message to alcoholics and to practice these principles in all our affairs.

I hasten to define "spiritual awakening," because many new people think they have to have a vision of God. AA defines spiritual awakening as "a psychic change sufficient to recover from alcoholism." That seems to mean, "We had our minds changed."

One of my favorite sponsors was Dick H., who was a Superior Court judge in Ventura County. I will close this chapter with a story Dick told on himself. I believe it completely summarizes the AA program.

"When I was sniffing around AA trying to decide if I really wanted to be sober, I rear-ended a truck up on the grapevine near Bakersfield. I was home recovering from my injuries when this fellow, Max, from AA came to my house every day. He brought in the mail, he picked up my kids at school, he acted like a personal valet. One day I said, 'Max, why do you do all this stuff for me?'

He said, 'You don't want to know.' So I continued to badger him until he agreed to tell me. I just knew he would say I would be a great asset to AA if I ever got sober.

Not so.

He said to me, 'I'll tell you why I do these things for you. I suffer from a terminal progressive fatal illness called alcoholism which will not yield to any human power. The only way I can get in touch with a superhuman power is to love and serve my fellow man at some cost to myself and with no expectation of reward. Nothing costs me more or offers me less expectation of reward than loving and serving you, you son of a bitch.'"

I call that Max's Prayer.

ART

I have been drawing and painting since I was very young. Over the years I have had some formal training, but very little. Most of my education has come from books, seminars, and experience.

Throughout my life, I have searched for a real definition of art. A character named Stephen Dedalus in James Joyce's book *A Portrait of the Artist as a Young Man* tried to define art as "the arrangement of the physical universe in such a way as to arrest the aesthetic sensibility." That is more of a description than a definition, but it's not too bad. I've never found a satisfactory definition of art, and so I've concluded that art is a subjective experience; it is in the eye of the beholder.

Once my friends Michael and Lucy and I were visiting the Los Angeles Museum of Art. There on the wall was a six-foot high white canvas covered with number-two pencil scribblings. My friends were "oohing" and "ahhing" over the canvas. I was saying, "This guy's pulling your leg."

They said, "You just don't get it."

They were right. I just didn't get it.

In a small book called *The Painted Word*, all about modern art, Tom Wolfe claims that there are fifteen thousand people creating modern art in a desperate attempt to avoid being bourgeois. Another fifteen thousand people are buying this stuff in a desperate attempt to avoid being thought bourgeois. I have visited art museums halfway around the world, in Paris, Rome, Venice, London, and Dublin, and in the United States in Los Angeles, San Francisco, and New York City. I can appreciate some modern art like Picasso's *Guernica* and his goat sculpture, but most of it eludes me entirely. I tend to favor the looser impressionistic paintings like those of Renoir and Monet, and some realistic paintings like those of Andrew Wyeth and Edward Hopper also appeal to me. In the end, I am convinced that a thing is art if you say it is.

Over the years, I have sold paintings and shown them a few times at shows. Several years ago, a Catholic nun I know asked me to paint a picture for her auction. I painted a dramatic portrait of Mother Teresa, whose name was the same as my friend, the nun. The painting sold at auction for five hundred dollars to a young couple who immediately gave the painting to Teresa, the nun. Teresa had it in her apartment until her death.

At one time at about age eighteen, I thought I might want to pursue art as a career. For a short time, I got a job with a commercial artist in Sioux City. Primarily we airbrushed photographs of farm machinery for newspaper ads. I became bored by this effort and moved on.

I've always had an ambivalent attitude about doing art. One of my male relatives said, "Only queers do that kind of work." Another relative said, "Art won't make the mare go." Because of these negative influences and lack of encouragement, I put art down for more than twenty years. Then in 1989, I was assigned to Dependency Court, where I dealt with severe child-abuse cases all day. The stress in that department was horrific. When I would drive my car under the courthouse in the morning, I could feel my body tightening up involuntarily.

To get relief from the stress, I found an art teacher and took up oil painting again. It was a life saver. When I am painting, my "monkey mind" is shut down completely. For me, painting is a true meditation. It has been a year since I have done any painting. When this book is finished, I will pick up my brushes once again.

RELIGION AND SPIRITUALITY

My earliest religious recollection is of a Father Huey threatening hellfire and damnation to the parishioners at the little St. Michael's Church in Leeds, Iowa. Their sin? Not putting enough money in the collection plate. It was a poor perish. My parents were more or less strict Catholics (Mother less so), which meant that we five children were required to attend Catholic schools, so I was enrolled at five years of age in the first grade at the Cathedral Grade School. Sister Clarissina, the tiny nun I mentioned earlier in my recollections, took a liking to me, and I soon warmed up to her. The first grade was my last positive experience in grade school.

The rest of grade school was a blur of fear and guilt. In fifth grade, I confessed to a crime I did not commit, throwing an eraser at the blackboard, to avoid being detained after school. I was ten miles from home and afraid I would not get there if detained.

By the time high school came around, I had become a full-blown rebel. My first year was spent at an all-boys high school called Trinity High School, run by the Marianist Brothers, who did not suffer fools or anyone else gladly.

During those growing up years, God became an angry old white guy in the sky who would drop you into a pool of everlasting fire for some damn small infractions. I learned to hate and fear this concept of God.

As a grownup, I went to Lourdes while traveling in France. This is the place where many miracles and cures have been reported. I did not go in the baths, because I did not believe I would be cured. I got drunk instead. As T. S. Eliot wrote, "I have heard the mermaids singing, each to each. I do not think that they will sing to me."

During three years of college, I did the bare minimum to stay a Catholic and less than that when I briefly (for one year) attended Creighton University School of Law. After Creighton and up to the time I married Mary Durkin, I barely met the requirements to stay in the church, and I did that mostly out of fear.

On September 10, 1971, I was attending a meeting of Alcoholics Anonymous in Beverly Hills when a gorgeous woman was giving a talk. As I have mentioned, I was immediately smitten with her beauty and personality, and after the meeting, I asked her out to coffee. We met at the Hamburger Hamlet on Wilshire Boulevard, had a lovely dinner, and started getting acquainted. It was her birthday, and she had her ten-year-old daughter, Ellen, with her. We began dating back and forth between Ojai, where I lived, and Westwood, where she lived, and after eighty-two days, we got married. Still believing that I was a Catholic, I felt the need to be married by a priest, even though Mary was out of the church having been divorced nine years earlier. I called my sister, Jean, and told her I needed to find a priest who would marry two people who could not legitimately marry in a Catholic church. She found a Father O'Neill, a Jesuit who was stationed in Watts. On a Saturday night, Mary and I went with our friends, Wilma and Click, down to Watts where Father O'Neill married us. That pretty much ended our relationship with the Catholic Church.

TRUST ALLAH, BUT TIE YOUR CAMEL

For about eighteen and a half years after I had my last drink, I held on to the very negative concept of God. He was to me still an angry old white guy in the sky. I hated and feared this concept of God, and after eighteen and a half years of sobriety, I finally let go of it. I let go of my belief in sin, guilt, and redemption.

For a while, I had no concept of God or higher power at all. Then one day I said to myself, "Lots of people who are sober claim to have a higher power, and they seem to be happy, joyous, and free. Perhaps you should find a higher power. You call yourself a judge; why don't you look at the evidence? Every day you see people who have come back from the gates of insanity and death to be restored to their rightful place in their homes, their professions, and society. You have seen gutter-crawling drunks recover and become respected members of society. Your friend Harold Hughes sobered up to become governor of Iowa."

The alcoholics I ran with said, "You can choose your own higher power, just so long as it makes sense to you."

Eventually I settled on a name given to God by the Lakota people. They refer to God as the Great Spirit, so I adopted that concept as one of my names for God. Over time, my concept of God has changed from a distant being in the universe to a presence within me. Jesus Christ said, "The kingdom of Heaven is within you," a concept I never heard when I was a churchgoer.

Today I pray every day at night. I thank the Great Spirit for one more day of sobriety, for one more day of life, and for my whole life, the good, the bad, and the ugly.

My spirituality tends toward the pragmatic. I like the Arab proverb, "Trust Allah, but tie your camel." A similar concept is expressed by the Apostle James: "Faith without works is dead." I have had a very hard life being disabled for sixty-seven years, but when I fully and completely accepted the fact that my life was hard and was always going to be hard, by the grace of God, it has gotten easy.

Finally, I have had a spiritual awakening as the result of taking the Twelve Steps of Alcoholics Anonymous, and I hasten to add that the spiritual awakening is defined by AA as "a psychic change sufficient to recover from alcoholism."

ACKNOWLEDGMENTS

I wish to thank Dr. David Richo, who first encouraged me to write this book. Also, I want to thank Cynthia Waring, my writing coach, who guided me through the process of writing. Many thanks to my superb court reporter, Leslie Spencer, who precisely took down every word of the book and helped in its creation in numerous other ways. Finally, but not least, I wish to thank Michael Armour, friend and professional writer, for his valuable insights.